WITHDRAWN

"Stories of disability are too few and too often told by non-disabled writers, but this collection's value goes far beyond representation. The wise, funny, heartbreaking, and joyful work in these pages can show any reader, disabled or not, how to navigate an unpredictable world."

James Tate Hill, author of *Blind Man's Bluff*

"'Nobody is ever out of the woods. Life is all about the woods,' Teresa Milbrodt explains in 'Cyclops Notes,' her nonfiction selection in this remarkable anthology of poetry and prose by thirty-three disabled writers. Each author guides the reader through the woods, along widely divergent paths of hope, fear, anger, humor, wisdom, patience, resignation. What they all have in common is the clarity and beauty of their writing. In 'pain(t)-by-number,' Lili Sarayrah tells us, '... when you see more than one side, speak more than one language, and know more than one kind of pain, you have trouble filling out forms.' This book won't help you fill out forms, but it will help you to confront and appreciate the complexities of life."

Joanne Durham, poet and author of *To Drink from a Wider Bowl*

"*In Between Spaces* is filled with unbridled vulnerability, searing empathy, and a sense of far-reaching hope. But more than anything, this is an anthology pierced through with beauty. I was left in tears of sadness and hope."

Tod Goldberg, New York Times bestselling author of *Gangsterland*, *Gangster Nation*, and *The Low Desert: Gangster Stories*

W 9-BJO-997

"*In Between Spaces* offers an immersive reading experience that highlights multiple ways of being a disabled person in the world. Through poetry, fiction, and nonfiction, the authors reveal and rip through shame and stigma to expose the 'frontal lobe like feathers of a bird' (Rob Colgate) and 'bruises like purple and yellow crocuses' (Natalie E. Illum). This anthology celebrates the power of difference with all of its messy and blurred edges, brain and pain fogs, and vibrating words that welcome us to move in whatever way available to the rich hum of this collection."

Stephanie Heit, author of *Psych Murders*

"This bold and moving anthology represents a wide variety of authors living with disability, offering a marvelous array of voices and using unique forms, styles, and points of view. Rendered with heart, humor, and truth throughout, *In Between Spaces* is an important and necessary contribution to the conversation around disability."

Elizabeth Crane, author of *This Story Will Change*

"Long overdue and awaited, *In Between Spaces* explores disability and difference with humor, frankness, and hard-fought wisdom."

Julija Šukys, author of *Siberian Exile: Blood, War, and a Granddaughter's Reckoning.*

"In this urgent collection, writers speak the unspeakable. From the shadows of disability, they reach beyond stigma, shame and silence to voice their lived truth: chronic panic, PTSD, mania, panic disorder, mobility struggles, seizures, cystic fibrosis, tachycardia, autism, bipolar, stuttering, blindness, hearing impairment, psychosis, and suicidal ideation. And they do so with bravery, pluck and honesty. In 'When My

Broken Brain Misfires,' essayist Vanessa Garza writes, 'I'm okay; I have to be.' As this anthology proves, she and her fellow writers are okay. By turns raw and polished, with both deft subtlety and hammer blows, *In Between Spaces* transforms our notions of 'other' into 'us.'"

Ethan Gilsdorf, teacher, poet, critic, author of *Fantasy Freaks and Gaming Geeks*, instructor of the GrubStreet Essay Incubator program

"*In Between Spaces* is a workout for the head and heart alike. Contributors play with form, mingle fact and fiction, and defy myths and preconceptions about disability with their wild, wise, and innovative work."

Trudy Lewis, author of *The Empire Rolls*

In Between Spaces

An Anthology of Disabled Writers

Edited by
Rebecca Burke

STILL
HOUSE
PRESS

All inquiries may be directed to:
Stillhouse Press
4400 University Drive, 3E4
Fairfax, VA 22030
www.stillhousepress.org

Stillhouse Press is an independent, student- and alumni-run nonprofit
press based out of Northern Viginia and established in collaboration
with the Fall for the Book festival.

Library of Congress Control Number: 2022932793
ISBN-13: 978-1-945233-15-9   (print)
ISBN-13: 978-1-945233-16-6   (electronic)

*For everyone who turned to books to
find themselves*

TABLE OF CONTENTS

Letter From the Editor

Dear reader,

You are holding in your hands the very first anthology published by Stillhouse Press. As a nonprofit, student-run teaching press, our students drive decisions about what we publish. From our readers to our editors, we empower students to make decisions about what they want to read and put out into the world. We strive to create work that reflects the diversity of our staff in their perspectives, experiences, and interests. *In Between Spaces* is both a culmination of this mission and the start of a new chapter for Stillhouse Press.

This collection was born out of lengthy discussions I led within our editorial board about diversity and accessibility in publishing. Discussions about how only 5 percent of all fiction books published since 1950[1] were written by people of color. Discussions about how disability representation is so often written by people who are not disabled, resulting in inaccurate, inauthentic, or stereotypical portrayals. Discussions about how marginalized people—Black people, Indigenous people, people of color, people with disabilities, people with mental illnesses, people who identify as gay, bisexual, transgender, nonbinary, pansexual, or asexual, those who have historically been silenced and pushed aside—deserve the space and platform to celebrate their voices, and as a small press not beholden

---

[1]   Based on data reported in "Just How White Is the Book Industry?" The New York Times. 11 December 2020. https://www.nytimes.com/interactive/2020/12/11/opinion/culture/diversity-publishing-industry.html

to marketing trends or profit margins, we have the platform and the responsibility to create these opportunities.

Growing up, I never read a book with a main character like me written by a disabled author. I was born with glaucoma in my right eye, only the second known case in a newborn at the time. The pressure in my eye was untreatable; it was removed when I was six weeks old, and I've worn prosthetics since. The back of my left eye is deformed, a result of a condition colloquially known as morning glory syndrome. Where the retina attaches to allow the information your eyes intake to be transmitted to your brain, my eye is dimpled and rough instead of smooth, my retina attached precariously by a sliver of tissue. At the time I was born, when my parents were navigating endless appointments at The Johns Hopkins Hospital without the expanses of the internet to turn to for information, every other person known to have this condition was blind. They were prepared for me to be as well. But I have sight. Remarkably good sight. While I lack depth perception and have reduced peripheral vision, I can read print, drive, wear glasses that correct the vision in my remaining eye to 20/30, all things we weren't sure I'd still be able to do by my mid-twenties.

My childhood was spent in this strange, liminal space—while I have never met the specifications to be legally blind, my vision loss affects every aspect of my life. As a child, I learned to read print quickly—I loved to read and tell stories, always immersing myself in different worlds— but my parents argued over whether I should learn braille. My annual doctor's appointments were filled with conversations I didn't understand; phrases like "coloboma," "detach retina," and "it's not a matter of if the worst will happen, but when it does" were imposed upon me at a young age. As best as anyone could explain it, that I had any sight at all was a medical anomaly. I should not expect my vision to last.

We turn to books to escape, to understand, to see ourselves reflected in someone else's words. There were no books for children like me.

No half-blind characters, no children in picture books waiting to have their prosthetic eyes cleaned, one eye socket sunken and empty, playing Tic-Tac-Toe with the specialist who sculpts and paints and cleans their prosthetics. As I grew older and developed a love for writing, my own characters suffered from this larger lack of representation. We become stronger writers by reading the work of others. But I had little to turn to for reference.

I struggled to write about vision loss without turning a piece into a lesson on ocular anatomy. In a narrative essay I turned in for a graduate school seminar in 2019, my classmates told me they were lost in the medical jargon. *Understandable*, I wrote in my notes. But how do I explain living with a condition no one else has? Other authors have done it. There are countless essays and memoirs about the experience of having a rare condition, but I struggled to connect with their work on the level I needed to produce my own.

During a Stillhouse editorial meeting in the fall of 2020, amidst a conversation about what this anthology could become, I said, "I have never read a book with a character like me." The conversation shuddered to a halt. From one Zoom panel to the next, I was met with blank stares and uncomfortable shifting. Publishing is not all-inclusive. It is an industry built upon cisgender, heteronormative, ableist, and white supremacist history. My admission was a confirmation of what we all knew. I certainly was not the first person to say this. I will not be the last.

When we opened submissions for this project, I wanted to invite work from anyone who identifies or has identified at some point in their lives as disabled, whatever that meant to them. Empowering our submitters to claim the label for themselves was critical to our process of developing this anthology. While we did not require individual pieces to be about disability, the authors who submitted seemed to embrace the opportunity to share their experience. I read over 200 pieces of fiction, nonfiction, and poetry alongside the incredible team of student and alumni editors and readers who volunteered to help. In every submission, I was blown away by the honesty and astuteness with which authors wrote about cerebral palsy, vision loss, hearing loss, limb difference, paralysis, chronic pain, chronic illness, depression, anxiety, bipolar disorder, autism, ADHD, and so much more. The work we read was urgent, necessary; each piece was a needed glimpse into the lived experiences of every author who shared their writing with us.

I was particularly struck by the volume of submissions we received about mental illness and neurodivergence, and the honesty with which these authors wrote about how their lives were impacted every day by conditions so often absent from conversations about disability and accessibility. Perceptions surrounding these conditions—autism, ADHD, and various learning disabilities as well as the broad spectrum of mental illnesses—are steeped in misconception and stigma. But these conditions impact every aspect of a person's life, just as visible physical disabilities do.

The work of these authors, in particular, found me at a time when I desperately needed it. During the process of editing this anthology, I was diagnosed with type II bipolar disorder and post-traumatic stress, diagnoses I've struggled to talk about, to engage with beyond my own tumultuous thoughts. For people close to me, this may be the first they've learned of my diagnoses, as I find writing about them easier. In many ways, being formally diagnosed cast aspects of my life in clarity for the first time. In other ways, it felt like I was spiraling wildly out of control. Just as when I was a child, I sought books and stories to lose myself in, characters or narratives I could relate to and use as a gateway to understand what these diagnoses meant for me. I devoured the work I found, the recommendations friends gave me, until I was once again empty-handed. Until I turned to our submissions queue. In these pieces, I found solace, community, and acceptance—the things I'd needed for so long. When my fellow editors presented their choices for this anthology, it was overwhelming to find that the same pieces I needed were also ones they felt they and others needed as well.

And still, perhaps even more than the wide array of conditions our authors covered, our team was captivated by how deftly they engaged with the intersections of disability with other identities, including race, queerness, class, and privilege. Disability, like any identity, is not singular or stagnant. People are never just one thing.

Even now, there is a pervasive school of thought that disabilities fit into narrow categories. If you use a wheelchair, you must not be able to walk at all. If you use a white cane, you must be completely blind. But this does not match reality. From mental to physical, visible to invisible, diagnosed to undiagnosed, the experiences of the thirty-three incredible authors within this book culminate in an authentically diverse exploration of what disability really is across poetry, fiction, and nonfiction. It exists in spaces in-between traditional diagnostic criteria and textbook definitions, where lived experience fills the gaps in our understanding. Whether congenital or developed later in life, chronic or ultimately temporary, experiencing life with a disability is multifaceted. It is joy and relief, heartache and fatigue. It is self-acceptance and empowerment. Within these pages, it is brought center stage: Disability is more expansive than many have ever considered.

Each piece in this book is deeply loved by the members of our editorial team. This anthology would not have been possible without their enthusiasm and commitment to our authors and their work throughout every stage of the process. Bringing a book to print takes a community, and I am so grateful for the one that came together to see this one into the world. To Meghan McNamara, and her fearless championing of this project in its early stages; to Amanda, Natalie, Lisa, Lee, Bareerah, Emilie, Hannah, Brittney, Reina, and Virginia, for their tireless work; to the entire editorial board at Stillhouse Press for their continued support; to the readers who helped with submissions; to the writers who submitted their work; and to the countless others who lent a moment of their time to make this book a reality: Thank you. This book would not exist without you.

My hope as you read is that you find yourself as enthralled as each of us were. For disabled readers, I hope you have an opportunity to find community within these pages, as I have. For nondisabled readers, I hope this book provides an opportunity to learn and empathize. Disabled people live rich, multifaceted, complicated lives. *In Between Spaces* reflects these lives and celebrates them.

Sincerely,
Rebecca Burke
Editor

Mornings

There was a time I could run. Not well, or willingly, and to be honest, I didn't really ever want to run—but the thing is if I wanted to, I could just put one foot in front of the other and it would work. *But you're not disabled. Disabled is—different.*

Some people wake up and lie in bed for a while and don't want to get up, and I'm like that too sometimes, but most days, I'm pretty much ready to get up, except one leg or the other is saying, "Wait, wait, wait, not now, who knows when, just not now."

I can ignore this, them, my legs. They're just these things below my torso; they don't own me. But then I slip them out from under the covers and swing them off the bed and they just hang there limp, loose, on fire. They knew I wasn't ready. Except it's been hours and it's time to feed the cat or dress for the meeting or I'm about to pee the sheets. *But you're not disabled. Disabled is—like really disabled.*

Sometimes when I'm crying I don't realize I'm crying, and people walk in and think something is wrong and hit me with the 'Oh my gosh are you okay what happened what's wrong' and nothing's wrong; it's just the excruciating pain making my eyes water, and sure, they look like tears and there's a slight lump in my throat and my head hurts if I don't drink one glass of water for every salty stream—but they're not tears. I used to think of them as tears too except I don't feel sad about it anymore so I'm not really crying—am I? *But you're not disabled—everyone has back problems.*

Some mornings I stand up and everything goes fine, and look at me, I'm walking to the bathroom and back and my legs haven't buckled, and

I can even do a little jig around the house —be careful in public or they'll think you're faking when you say you need to work remotely.

Today, there's that nice overcast sky I love, and I want to move closer to the window to lift my face up into the sunny-but-not-blinding light. I'm no longer sleepy so there's no point lying here. Besides, the cat hasn't been fed yet, and I think I have to pee again. But, "Wait, wait, wait, not now, not yet."

Jess Skyleson

Birdhouse

Let me tell you a story.
My wife once worked with this guy (I can't remember his name,
let's call him Al), who got into a terrible car accident. Really, it was a miracle
he even survived. He had a serious head injury, though,
and needed rehabilitation. So there he was at the hospital, re-learning how
to use his hands, when they gave him some pieces of wood—
told him to try building a birdhouse,
like the one shown on the paper. He had never done any woodworking before,
but figured, *Why the heck not*, and gave it a shot. He built that little birdhouse,
then another, and another. He said he just started seeing birdhouses,
really intricate designs, like little birdmansions, inside of his mind—
said he could even walk through them, exploring those tiny rooms
like an avian Frank Lloyd Wright, knowing just where to place each floor,
the best angles for the roof, the door. Of course the birds flocked
to them, but people did too, amazed that someone who hadn't known
how to nail two boards was somehow creating art,
winning awards. Then one day, after he became
nearly accustomed to this bit of fame, he said his visions of birdhouses
suddenly stopped. His thoughts returned
back to unfinished wood, the bright paint peeling off, fading away. Today,
you would never know he was anything
other than just a regular guy. I really wish I could remember his name,
but you see, after the chemo, I started living
inside a much smaller brain.

Confessions of a Reluctant Zebra

"When you hear hoofbeats in the night, look for horses—not zebras."
—Dr. Theodore Woodward

I can see the teapot from my bed, about ten steps away, another eight to the bathroom.
Normally this sort of information would be of little interest to me, but more recently,
my world has gotten very small.

In fact, most days my world is not much bigger than the six-by-four-foot bed I've been relegated to. It's not a bad bed, really. It's clean, comfortable. Yet, it's becoming dangerously close to defining the parameters of my existence.

And that's the problem.

Come to think of it, I never really would have spent much time thinking about beds at all.
But then again, why would I?

Still, beds are rather amazing, don't you think? Each possesses a unique history all its own—in which lives are conceived and lost, vows are made, promises broken and spirits renewed.

But back to the bed that concerns me most, my bed.

So here I am, having spent days, weeks, months (years) in this bed plotting my escape.

But illness demands more than a floor plan when it comes to successful egress.

Anyway, lying here horizontally seems to lend itself more to dreams and metaphors than to pragmatic agendas.

Like today, if I wasn't stuck in the supine position, I never would have thought twice about that spider on my ceiling. I probably wouldn't have even noticed it was there. Instead, I have spent considerable time in the wee hours of this crisp, December morning considering the fate of a little bug that made a wrong turn and somehow ended up here.

And I found myself identifying with an insect stuck in a spider's spindly web.

Because I do feel trapped in a circumstance that seems devoid of anything remotely certain, most importantly, a future. Of course, it's my life I'm rooting for, and my glimpse of freedom that I must hold onto.

And I try to hold onto dreams, too, beautifully woven, tightly wrapped; those forgotten gifts that allow the soul to breathe once more.

Is it better to dream in color, or not to dream at all?

I don't know. I'm beginning to wonder if dreams are merely a luxury reserved for those living in the well world.

For now, these drifting thoughts weave in and out, like billowy, marshmallow clouds, hovering just above the surface of my make-shift entombment, as I try to imagine life outside the front door, just 12 steps away.

But I still believe it's possible for that little bug to disentangle itself from the spider's proverbial web, even though the odds may seem dramatically against it.

Of course, it's my life I'm rooting for, and my glimpse of freedom that I must hold onto.

And I try to hold on to the promise of tomorrow, which will surely arrive as it did today, in all its glory and splendor, as the winter's night sky begins to peel back and opens wide, light pours in, enveloping the earth like warm butterscotch.

Illumination.

Anticipation.

Resignation.

We begin again.

Becca Carson

Health History

When I was a kid, I used to slip underwater in the tub and stare straight up
at the ceiling, eyes unblinking and lungs stinging for as long as I could
because underwater was the only place in my house I could hear
my own heartbeat and feel
relieved to still have one

and maybe that is why every time
we spent Saturdays in June at the outdoor pool
I scraped my palms trying to hold on to
the rough cement bottom of the deep end
even knowing the consequences
even knowing my little sister would be running to tattle on me
for trying to drown myself, to claw my way back home,

and maybe to you this is not the same as swimming in
benzodiazepines and stimulants but I
know what the bottom feels like
with everyone else muffled, so far away
and I don't have to be submerged to
notice my heart flutter kicking to the surface of the silent
white flesh of my stomach when they ask me to hold *extra still*
in the doctor's office and I've gotten good at stillness but
to answer your question, no.
I don't remember when it all started.

pain(t) — by — number

Every time my brush touches paper, I am in pain. I think this is because I buy the most elaborate paint-by-number in an effort to reclaim my childhood joy but instead manage to fuel my adult angst. In reality, my new pain began in earnest several months ago, and now that it is escalating, I am beginning to panic. I haven't even recovered from my last surgery yet. That surgery eased the stomach pain, but this pain spreads through my back and down my left leg, slow and sticky as molasses. I will become obsessed with not only finding a satisfying diagnosis but understanding why it happened to me and so soon, as if I have a certain allotment of pain to meet like an insurance deductible. Eventually it will be chalked up to "bad luck" because of a series of supposedly unrelated and oddly specific issues. For some reason, right now I think this painting will be the perfect distraction. It is massive and some of the shapes are so tiny, each miniature printed number barely fits inside. The reviews claim it takes forty to fifty hours of work to complete, but it will take me almost as many weeks.

I later learn the painting is a pirated copy of *Rain's Rustle* by Leonid Afremov. It pictures a tree-lined street on a rainy evening. Lamplight reflects off pools of water. There are two figures covered by an umbrella who are shadowy blobs, giving more the impression of instability than forward motion. This feels appropriate. It seems like a depiction of late fall or early winter, but when I open the paints, they are surprisingly primary colored.

If my pain were a color, it would be like paint No. 19, a shade of orange like those traffic cones marking caution ahead. It is now July in Knoxville, Tennessee, and the heat and humidity are oppressive. I settle on the porch screened in from the slow burning of the world that is 2020. The cicadas chatter away in ecstasy, competing with the incessant cackling of the blue jays. I'm surprised that up close a bird call coming from a tiny tuft can be this aggressive, so loud that it's almost confrontational. At this point I can still stand, so I get my violin out to try and imitate them. I can hear Baba doing a better job as he whistles in the garden. He has years of practice. He talks to the birds more than he talks to anyone else because they forgive him every time.

I start painting with the canvas precariously pinned to a cardboard box balanced on an easel of my late grandpa's that I found cleaning out the basement. The description reassures that "it doesn't need any basic knack of painting." The tiny numbers are an intricate map to nowhere.

Thanks to the unbearable combination of the pain and the pandemic, my outings are restricted to clinics and offices where people keep asking me for my pain level on a scale of 1 to 10. They do this briskly, as if asking about the weather. My first thought is that I wonder which numeral system they mean. Do they know that in English we use the Arabic numeral system, although in Arabic a different system is used entirely, and is even written in the opposite direction? I want to tell them that when you see more than one side, speak more than one language, and know more than one kind of pain, you have trouble filling out forms. To me, the fact that they use base 10 proves that the metric system is better. Sometimes I qualify my pain level partially based on how much attention I want to be given. I find it odd that the top of the pain scale means it's bad enough to go to the ER. I remember my ER trips involved varying levels of agony, so which time do they mean?

The first person who offers me the pain scale also lets me know that I am too young for this pain and he is praying for me. His church group is still meeting on Zoom and they would love to have me. I stare at him wordlessly until he backs out of the room slowly. I am disappointed because this waiting room doesn't even have a Bible lying in wait. Beware the power of the converted.

It is now August and my pain is climbing with the temperature. At first, I stand while painting but soon I find myself forced to sit. For an MRI with contrast dye, I am introduced to the first of many very, very long needles and am told to relax as it pushes into me like an eager lover. Fluid fills my hip and the pain instantly increases. My feet are bound together so the machine can capture a picture at the right angle. For the next few weeks, the pain is so intense it has brought me to my knees or, more accurately, flat on my back, so I paint awkwardly propped up wearing a bib. Now, I am in a state of permanent recline. This might sound somewhat refined until you realize I am an open display of vulnerability. Ice packs sandwich my body from my back down to my left ankle, so that I shiver in the sweltering heat.

In September, I want to pick a number to paint based on my pain, except these numbers go up to 22. This range seems more realistic for my pain's temperament. I settle on 12. As I clean my brush, watching a serene blue pool and dissipate, I think about how chronic pain means I can't decide if I have a higher pain threshold because I'm used to it, or a lower pain threshold because the new pain is added onto the old. I become like that GIF of the woman surrounded by a million equations, deep in impossible calculations.

On a bright morning when I can feel the seasons changing, I dip my brush in 8, a dark brown for a twisting tree trunk. As my brush drags along the canvas, painting just slightly outside the lines, I wonder if emotional pain counts as a part of my equation. Pain is interpreted by the brain, and I want to know how it sifts one type of pain from the other or if it even knows the difference.

Apparently, pain + avoidance = suffering. A simple equation that takes a lot of figuring. This means that pain is not the problem, suffering is. My mom asks how I'm feeling and I say irritated. She laughs and says she means how is my pain today. I think she should be more specific. After an hour of painting, I swear it looks exactly the same.

So far, I have been tossed around between doctors like a hot potato. I feel in-between a lot of the time. Specifically in-between cultures, jobs, and diagnoses. I try to lighten the mood by referring to my health history as a series of maladies. Technically, only five organs are required to live, but it worries me that we know that. On the bright side, I've only had two organs removed, down to seventy-six. Is that more or less than you would have guessed?

My body is both incredible and fallible. I mourn the version of me who never even thought about my left leg except to assess its size. As I put down my brush to stretch out my cramping arm, it occurs to me that at this exact moment some other internal part of me could be approaching its tipping point. I cross-examine my seemingly innocent right shoulder. It has nothing to say. I can't control any of this, so instead I focus on sunscreen.

At my next appointment, a tall, confident spine specialist unnervingly describes a potential surgery like shooting a fox. "We can hear rustling in the bushes," he says, "we know something's coming, but we don't want to shoot too soon. What if we aren't in the right spot?" He apologizes for the violent imagery. I think of this months later when an actual fox starts screaming outside my log cabin window and sounds like a cross between a crying baby and a goose being murdered.

In October, the scene outside my screened-in porch begins to match my patchy painting. Instead of being able to count on moving, I now count my steps. When the light is too far away to turn off, I leave it burning like my nerves. My carbon footprint is now more prominent than my footsteps. The skin on my back has become so sensitive that when my mom tries to hug me, I yelp.

When I manage to get an appointment with a hip specialist in Nashville, I am sure that he will be my Messiah. Instead, he describes my situation as being at the bottom of a laundry basket with many layers of clothes piled on top of me. "We have to peel away the layers to find the source." If we operate now, with this level of nerve pain, I will never recover. This odd metaphor cycles in my head as my mother drives the three hours home and I brace against every bump in the road. When I get inside, I am so angry that I want to throw the small blue and white speckled glass vase I love, the one that fits so soothingly in my palm, but instead settle on my value bottle of Tylenol Extra Strength. It pops open and white pills explode everywhere like somber confetti. When I can't pick them up, I cry so hard I'm surprised that I don't pass out.

The specialist has suggested a new medication which I add to my dizzying array. Grammy tells me I am making a mistake while simultaneously pushing miracle pills on me. Correlation is not causation so neither of us can be sure who's right. In desperation I start chanting every day, feeling both ancient and insane. I now sing "I am heaaaaalinggggg" to myself in the car on the way to physical therapy.

During my fourth MRI, I whisper that I love myself over and over again. Inside the white, coffin-like structure I wear thick, padded headphones to protect my hearing. The technician asks if I am comfortable. This is hilarious. Soon the machine rumbles and shoots around me like a sterile battlefield, the powerful magnets performing what seems to me like noisy, inelegant magic to capture detailed images of my insides. You would think for this kind of money a handy body-wide map would be produced, but no, the MRIs of my lower back, pelvis, and two of my left hip each warranted separate occasions. I try to deepen my breath and picture myself on a beach vacation.

My therapist says, "healing is not linear," and now I wonder the same about pain. Is it cyclical? Is it more like one step forward and two steps back? Like some kind of fucked up cha-cha? What about when you can't walk, much less dance? At my lowest point, I decide to listen to one new song each day and add it to a playlist. For the duration of the song, I move in whatever way I can. Sometimes this means twitching a toe.

By Thanksgiving, it becomes too cold to reasonably lie on the porch anymore and I am moved inside. At first, I paint often by the window, propped up on a blush-colored loveseat, then weeks guiltily pass, and now I have given up altogether. The painting is frozen in a state of disarray like me. My grandpa's easel is folded up and the cardboard box the painting is attached to is for some reason now suspended on my music stand, both of them gathering dust in the corner. They join my violin in the room of things I can't do anymore.

In December, I notice the paints have dried up although the pain hasn't, so I fret over how to order a new set. I worry that the signals in my brain are also drying, settling in their grooves, molding new pathways. At the beginning of the pandemic, I had crisscrossed the neighborhood like a caged animal, racking up miles. Over time, I found myself struggling to make it a block. Now I write a poem to each leg, dedicating one to the left and one to the right. I don't notice until someone points out that I have forgotten to claim them. Whether I want them or not, they are not "the" legs, they are "my" legs.

My writing comes out disjointed: my figure has flaws, my flaws figured me out long ago. These hips don't lie but damn they hurt (Shakira Shakira). In Arabic, Shakira means "thankful," but unfortunately, I'm not. I no longer fantasize about other bodies but rather about my own in movement. I read once that creative acts are a way to soothe pain, but this confuses me because my greatest act of creation is the pain itself.

My progress, or rather my deterioration, is measured by the street I live on, by if I can walk down to the stop sign and back. My personal pain-by-number box. By January, I can't make it anywhere near the stop sign, so I'm surprised when I drive past it one day to see that the entire house at the end of the street is gone, the earth torn up like my expectations. Is that a sign?

In February, I capitulate and plan to have another surgery in March. Surrender in Arabic is إستسلام, and I am delighted to realize that it ends with سلام, meaning peace. I decide that surrender is not the same as giving up but rather a roundabout acceptance. Maybe it's not surrendering to anything, but simply surrendering what was.

Now I know I have a bone malformation in both hips. The kicker: only one has symptoms. The other one could start, just not now. No "why." Just "is." A surgery to fix the left hip, but what about the right one? The surgeon and I will both initial skin with Sharpie so they cut the right one. I'm looking forward to the drama, but in reality, all that happens is that at least seven different people verbally confirm which leg is being cut every time we interact. It happens so many times that the word "left" starts to sound made up and I worry about my pronunciation. Behind double masks in the hospital, I sit and think that really, it's more like three masks, the KN-95, the cloth one on top, and the carefully arranged features I wear to reassure everyone that this is all normal.

As I wait for the anesthesiologist, I quietly sing "you are safe, you are safe, you are safe," even though there's a pandemic on and in March of 2021, we don't all have access to vaccines yet and objectively no one is safe. I wonder why sometimes my chants start with "I" and sometimes with "you." Who am I addressing?

When I wake up from the surgery, I want to go right back to sleep because of the pain, so I am put on a Fentanyl drip and am alarmed by how much I like it. At home, I lie inside a barricade of pillows to keep my leg from turning out. Alarms are set for every four hours to keep on top of the pills. I am exhausted. At twenty-nine, I have had one extended hospital stay and four surgeries, which is less than some and more than many, including Grammy who is now ninety-six. She is radiant and energetic and leans jauntily on her cane. I cling desperately to my crutches.

Physical therapy is even more of a balancing act now as I slowly increase the weight bearing on my left leg. This leads to more confusing calculations, as in, how does one determine putting only 25 percent of one's weight on one leg? Exercises and pills and excruciating stretches become a blur. When we watch *Groundhog Day*, it feels familiar but seems like Bill Murray gets to have much more fun than I do. As I get stronger, I dust off my unopened paint set and start again. My method is haphazard, determined by which part of the canvas is most accessible. I listen to audiobooks and disappear in the details until my thumb cramps in protest.

In April, my caring physical therapist determines it's time to ditch the crutches. This feels abrupt because they are my closest friends. I picture the staples holding the cartilage to my hip socket popping out. I imagine the newly shaved femur snapping under my weight. Suddenly, there are only a few blobs left to paint. I find myself perversely slowing down, stretching out my experience on this canvas. I put it up close to my face and scan it from corner to corner, finding minuscule patches I have forgotten that I conquer with dripping glee. Some of the lighter colors really do need a second coat... now it feels done.

When I finish the painting, I am both in awe and overwhelmingly sad. The countdown is complete. I realize that the ten months of the painting correspond to that stupid pain scale. It is tempting to pair each month with a number, but the pain was in no way on some kind of steady decline. Waning and growing on its own schedule, it is still courting me and stalking me and preying on me, but now I am stronger. When I look at my painting, I see that some of the numbers are showing through the paint, and I like that. It is a statement of my acceptance of the imperfection, a way to feature the process. I am surprised to have spent so much time on a project only in service of myself, for no particular or discernible reason except to keep myself living. I put away my pain(t) and when we film my first wobbly steps, no one's counting.

Latif Askia Ba

On Gospel (a Meander)

Nor is there pain, or cause of pain,
Or cease in pain, or noble path
To lead from pain.
—*"The Heart Sutra" as recited in the Triratna Buddhist Community*

Tomorrow morning,

I will struggle to get out of bed,

finding the weight of the covers

against my crooked glowing limbs

formidable.

My aide will wait

as always

for the moment

to crush my food with a spoon

and cram the mush down my throat.

It's a peculiar feeling:

quivering naked on the shower floor,

my boney ass on the wet tiles

as I wait for her to roll in my chair.

This is my life. My days pastel.

The substances offset nothing—

kicking a can down the road,

a demonstrating monk.

I listen to Aretha's gospel

over and over—she shows me how to pray,

how to hang one's head,

how to shake and bow,

to rattle and bend, to quake and cry.

I hear her conjure up her lord

in bejeweled robes from the intricacies

of her throat. I hear the congregation
testify: shouting out a Socratic oath,
that of a question in the shadow of a statement.
I know she stood as high as Homer
and reached out in the dark,
and pulled out something from nothing.
She baptized the iambic flesh of Dr. Watts
in the black blood-rills of the sudden-dead.
She dug out fossilized fetters from the Mississippi scars.
And that old man river flows
through war and antebellum,
its ancient schools and wild gardens
waiting to become bank, bed, or delta.
Will the pupils find rest
after deposition? Will the flowers
squirm into sunlight? Will they
pass on their genes and testify?

It's so peculiar
being broken in an obvious way.
Most people can hide it
under ironed plaid
and vacant smiles.
Only lovers can dig it
out of them and
treat it like an ugly dog
or leave it like a baby,
the Nile rocking his basket.
I cannot hide—
this body like an exile,
like a wound dumb luck carved into my neurons,
a wound only words can pass through.

Paper planes ripped from Plato's Republic
and the Pali Canon collide with verses
of Patwah. Only the gospel can remedy
this confusion: the black savage in me
bending his burly neck to the holy word.
In secret, she recognizes it. In secret,
she remembers. In secret,
she knows the trinity
that they tried to bind her with
was forged in the volcanic crucible
of negritude. In secret,
she holds court with Jesus
and delivers his gospel
from the gullies of her lungs. In secret,
she laughs at those iron-spine priests. She knows
one must bend to testify.

Cynthia Romanowski

Live Action Regret

The new boyfriend picks you up for dinner. He is talking about his boss and you're trying to figure out how to tell him that you're crazy. That you were crazy. Are crazy? And not in the wild-drunken-sorority-girl way but rather in the federal-government-sends-you-checks kind of way.

The restaurant is nice, so you are instantly uncomfortable. The menu is a fusion of two ethnic foods you've never tried. The new boyfriend is talking about taxes, how his mother works for the IRS. It couldn't be more boring than this, but you forgive him because you like him. The thought itself, *I like him*, makes you nervous and excited. You might really like someone for once.

You decide the new boyfriend looks handsome, there in the low light—big ears, receding hairline, small teeth, but still, somehow, he is handsome. And you are smiling. Pretending to listen.

*

It's November, which means you've been stable on medication for exactly five years, sixty months, though it's not something that people really celebrate. It's not like remission from cancer or sobriety. Nobody celebrates *not* being put in a mental hospital. People might celebrate getting out of a mental hospital. Maybe. But after being out, most people try to pretend like it never happened.

*

The new boyfriend wants to know about your day. If you like spicy foods. Do you follow sports? Politics? Have you watched *Mad Men*? Do you ever smoke meth? Just kidding, the new boyfriend would never ask you that. You wonder what the new boyfriend's meth equivalent is, what he looked like at his lowest point.

*

Sixty months. Five years. You recognized the milestone earlier today at the gynecologist. She started with a question: Is there anything I need to know?

You told her about one STD. Then, slowly, a second STD. The ones diagnosed at Planned Parenthood forever ago, when you were still a girl. She typed them into her computer.

"This says you have Medicare. That can't be right. You're too young."

"I do, I'm on disability for bipolar disorder."

"You're lucky. That's hard to get."

"You mean like, hard to get for having mental problems?"

"Yes."

You don't know whether or not she put the two things together, the bipolar disorder and the permanent sexual infections. You try to believe there's a link. Most of the time though, the word *slut* just echoes in your head. Reverberating, pounding like a heartbeat. Slut. Slut.

Therapists have tried to teach you to separate the behavior from who you are. How to convince yourself that you are not a lazy fuck, a whore, a flake, an egomaniac. They tell you, you're a decent person. You try to believe it.

"Have you ever been hospitalized?" the gyno asks.

"Yes, a few times."

*

The new boyfriend is eating and talking while there is still food in his mouth. Maybe you won't tell him these things about you tonight. Maybe it's still too soon. Maybe you won't ever tell him.

*

Earlier today, after the exam, the gyno squeezed your arm and it made you want to cry. She said you were doing good. That you had been through a lot. That five years stable for someone your age is impressive.

In ten minutes the new gyno knew more about you than the new boyfriend might ever know.

*

Now he's ordering dessert, but all you want is another drink and a cigarette. You feel like an imposter in your own life. A bad actress playing a character she can't relate to. He's asking how you take your coffee, if you like chocolate more than caramel and do you want to come over?

Yes, you do.

*

After the gyno, you did cry. Alone in your car in broad daylight. No matter how stable, there are consequences for past transgressions. There are maxed out credit cards, college transcripts filled with F's and W's. There are years lost, lapses in employment that raise questions. There is arrested development. Metastasized anxiety. Side effects. There are family members haunted by your actions, friends that won't talk to you anymore, fears real and imagined.

*

In the parking lot the new boyfriend is opening your car door. The roads are shiny and slick with rain. He's driving fast and you're wishing you were drunk. He holds your hand for a little while before placing it near his inner thigh. You take this as a hint and go down on him before he can ask. For you it's a simple expression of gratitude, your version of *thanks, I had a nice time.*

*

Earlier today you cried in your car and then you cried in the shower and then you smoked a joint. You remembered walking with no shoes on in the city. How people looked at you. How they looked past you. You remembered how your hair had to be chopped off, how it was matted like a stray dog's. Then you thought about what normal means.

*

Rain is beating down on the new boyfriend's car. He swerves into the next lane when he comes. You move off of him, wipe your mouth with the back of your hand. The car is steady again, moving faster as you both stay silent in the dark. That's when the shame hits. The new boyfriend looks confused when you ask him to take you home.

By the time he's parked at your place the rain has already stopped. In front of your apartment the new boyfriend is squeezing your hand.

"You didn't have to do that," he says.

"It's nothing."

"It's not nothing."

You nod. For the third time today, you blink back tears.

The new boyfriend has seen more of you than you realize. He wraps his arms around you.

While he lingers at your front door, you think about time. How the next month will be sixty-one months. How next year will be six years. Someday, you will say the things you need to, but for now you can only say goodnight.

Zackary Medlin

My Mania as an Alaskan Summer

like watching the dark
never darken past the blue
burn of an alcohol flame
igniting the purple bloom
in the fields of fireweed
stretched across the land
like a lavender perfume
wafting off a someone
you want to dance with
slowly tongue to tongue
in tiny untying circles
when three drinks in
at a party where everyone is
charming & smitten with new
like a third act in a teen
comedy where a beauty is
recognized to be sumptuous
without her glasses
it's hard to see a thing
save this innumerable neon
light spilled on a rain-glossed
street like a gasoline puddle
prettied to rainbow by sun
I'm a match to strike
& flick into the fuel

action-movie-like
watch the flame leap lurid
bursting out of existence
the smoke snaking itself
into itself an uroboros
blurring into the inevitable
far darkness to come

Management Problems

"You were starving," my mom said.

"They wouldn't believe me. They blamed me."

"I picked up the phone and called up Dr. Warwick and said, 'Take her. I can't do it anymore.' And you know what he did, Tessa, he was such a good man. He said, 'We will take her as long as you need.'"

"The thing is, Tessa," my mom continued, "I was feeding you eight to ten hours a day. Your father was working all day. You just kept spitting and vomiting everything up. No one believed me. They said it was 'management problems.' I will tell you management problems—you try and feed a baby for that many hours and not go crazy."

"You were so skinny, Tessa. No one wanted to hold you. They were too afraid they would hurt you."

"I didn't come see you for five days. Your-dad-went-every-day."

Her throat started to throttle, deep inhales; her voice began to vibrate with a whistle of her throat narrowing. "I just couldn't. They were judging me. I-left-you." She bawled and sobbed into the phone, "They were judging me. I-left-you."

*

I sighed. I could see her red nose and flushed cheeks, her wiping her tears away with the back of her hand. I could see her tears before her smiles. I set the phone down gently on the receiver. What did she do for those five days? Did she sit alone in silence? Did she call her friends? Did she sit in her nightgown and not go out? Did she shower or cry? Who is my mother?

My mom's life has always played out in scenes, moments, threats. She wanted us, my brother, Andrew, and me, to know her life, and yet not know it at all. As soon as we started to possibly know where she came from, to understand who she was, she said, "You don't know my life. No one knows my life." The door shut; cupboards slammed. She would sit with her legs crossed tight. She would sit and doodle for hours while watching TV, talking on the phone, or in silence. She would push her upper lip against her lower, a scorned pout.

Then my childhood story came in scenes, moments, and threats:

"You were very sick."

"Nobody wanted to pick you up, afraid they would hurt you, but I picked you up. I held you."

"As soon as I had you, they took you."

"Your father followed the ambulance."

"You weighed nine pounds at nine months."

"They blamed me."

"We are not mean people."

I was the child who absorbed all her words. They would touch my skin and then my heart. I took them in and absorbed all her cries until I had to shut them out.

As I got older, I wanted to make sense of her words, although in some ways I was afraid. I wanted to fill in the gaps, the phrases and the moments. I wanted to slide together the pieces and understand what happened.

When I was twenty-two years old, I worked for the Children's Minnesota Hospital – Minneapolis in the medical records department. I handled old files, old mold pressed tight, giving off the waft of that sweet, musky smell. I looked up my file name, and I had three admissions in microfiche, which I printed.

I had been receiving care at the University of Minnesota hospital and had been for as long as I could remember. I requested my medical records for the first five years of my life and three more admissions. These records were spotty, but I started to peel back the dates.

*

Admission to Children's Hospital August 13, 1977 – August 24, 1977: Tessa Weber is a 36-38-week female infant born at 7lbs. 10oz. at Mercy Hospital in Anoka found to have meconium peritonitis and ileal atresia. She was transferred to Children's Hospital NICU at one day old and her ileal atresia was repaired the next day. The family history reveals a paternal first cousin with juvenile diabetes mellitus, no history of cystic fibrosis.[1]

Meconium peritonitis is rupture of the bowel before birth, and ileal atresia is complete obstruction.

*

Admission to Mercy Hospital September 13, 1977 – September 15, 1977: Failure to thrive and poor weight gain; very skinny baby who is nonetheless alert and active. The pediatric surgeons felt that lack of weight gain was understandable because of the ileal dilation at surgery. Discharged. Follow-up with pediatrician one week later and then every two weeks until weight gain is noted.[2]

---

[1] At one day old, I was transferred from Mercy Medical Center to Minneapolis Children's Hospital. I had emergency surgery to remove a portion of my bowel, meconium peritonitis (bowel perforation) and ileal atresia (blockage in ileum of intestine). A strong indication of cystic fibrosis. The family history revealed "no history of cystic fibrosis" (CF). CF was in question, and a sweat test was performed (common test for cystic fibrosis). The result was negative. Babies often do not produce much sweat; therefore, an inaccurate result.

[2] ADM: 9/13/77, DIS 9/15/77
Second admission at Mercy Medical Center. My weight at birth was 7lbs. 10 oz. At this admission, 6lbs. 6 oz. "Failure to thrive" was noted. Normal white blood count (WBC) is 4,000 – 10,000. My WBC was 16,800. Not normal. "Sweat chlorides are pending, although, they were normal when done at Minneapolis Children's Hospital." They were questioning CF again.

The admissions and a catalog of appointments dates continued. I sat down and decided to write. I realized I was a writer when the more I wrote, the more life made sense. "I hate it when you write," my mom always said.

*

Clocks. When sitting alone, I am hyper aware of clocks. The ticking of clocks. The size, volume, and rhythm they keep. We had two grandfather clocks in our house. Every fifteen minutes, they chimed, a higher pitch than the half-hour chime. Then the big masterful chime—its own clockwork song on the hour, every hour. Both of the grandfather clocks were in sync, perfect pitch on time.

My mom was like a clock, a Father Time grandfather clock. The small hand made a tiny tick; tick, tick, tick, tick. One too many ticks, my mom hit. She slammed cupboard doors and drawers. The glass and silverware shook, one door after the next. My chest cavity rattled from the vibrations. You couldn't move; afraid you may be hit. "If I could, I would hit you so hard it would make your head spin," she would say.

She never hit us. Actually, that's a lie. She never hit us with her hand. I was only hit with the belt a couple of times. My brother got the wooden spoon until she broke it. We had just finished mixing peanut butter cookies and had put the first batch in the oven. The whiff of slowly rising peanut butter dough was filling the kitchen while I sat on the steps and watched through the wooden spindles as my mother hit my brother. The broken wooden piece dropped, and my mother's hand released

---

Pg. 2: "The pediatric surgeons felt that the lack of weight gain was understandable because of the ileal dilatation at surgery. They believed weight gain will begin within the next three months." They were questioning CF again.

CF affects the lungs or the lungs and pancreas, depending on mutation. My mutation affects the lungs and pancreas. I was absorbing next to nothing for food intake.

from his belt loop and jeans. He ran, crying. His door slammed. The oven timer beeped.

My mom ran down the stairs past me, thump, thump, thump, thump, all the way down. Bam! She slammed her bedroom door. I stood and climbed up the stairs. I walked over to the oven, put the gloves, fire engine red, over my hands and took the cookies out. I stood, listening to her sobs—again. The kitchen was above their bedroom, and I could hear every inhale and blubbery exhale.

Standing there, I felt that sting in my heart. I was sad hearing her cry. I was sad hearing my brother cry, but I was angry for him, too. I didn't want to touch that stupid spoon, lying there in the corner. My dad would be home from work soon.

"What is going on here?" he asked. My brother and I said nothing. My mom opened the bedroom door, the sound of a suction released. She walked up the steps; each foot shook the ground. She slid into a kitchen chair. My father placed his hand on her shoulder. She covered her face with her hands and cried and bawled some more.

*

I went ahead and typed up my questions, seventeen in total. I typed no more than two questions on each white sheet, allowing for space; clarity; to know.

I packaged up the papers and put them in a large white envelope, addressed to my mom and dad. The last time I sent an envelope to my mom, she put the envelope I sent her unopened inside a larger envelope. She sealed it with a red magic marker smiley face she drew and sent it back to me. This time I gave them a heads up what it was, telling them not to be concerned. My mom routinely and cyclically said, "We are not mean people, Tessa." Grandma was mean; Mom was not. I took a breath in, and off it went.

Question 1:

Me: *Mom, how long did you stay in the hospital after I was born?*

Mom: *One night and I was able to leave and be w/ you at Children's the next day.*

Question 2:

Me: *Right after I was born, when I was transferred to Children's, was it just Dad that came with?*

Mom: *Yes.*

Question 3:

Me: *After my initial stay at Children's, was I transferred to the University after that point?*

Mom: *No, you came home w/ us. The U was way down the line (so to speak).* I was transferred because I had an obstruction and needed immediate surgery.

Question 4:

Me: *Was Dr. Warwick the first pediatrician you met up with at the University? Did I start seeing him right away after my operation at Children's?*[3]

Mom:

1st question: *We first met w/ an intern.*

2nd question: *No – that was nine months later, when you were finally diagnosed.*

*

---

[3] Dr. Warren Warwick – University of Minnesota faculty 1960-2011. Passed February 15, 2016. Inventor of the percussive vest (CF vest). I would not be here without Dr. Warwick. His patience and kindness; persistence for knowledge, "clarity and force." Heart.

My mom always said that 'we were lucky.'

"I looked at Grandma, right before leaving for school, and she snatched my glasses off my face and threw them on the floor. They broke," she said.

'We were lucky.'

"Grandma came after me with a knife. I ran to my room as fast as I could and slammed the door. I waited until she left for work, and then I left with nothing but clothes on my back." She always slowed down the last half of the sentence, to make it stick. 'I-left-with-nothing-but-the-clothes-on-my-back.'

I am sure she did. Who am I to question? Did you leave with nothing-but-the-clothes on-your-back? What did you wear? Did you take food? How long did you walk? Did you go to a friend's house?

I wondered, did Grandma open the silverware drawer and grab the serrated knife and walk towards my mom one solid step at a time, or was it hurried with spit flying out of her mouth? Was the knife pointing up, or did she try to play the part—allowing her hand to grip the knife and have it facing halfway down as if she was going to stab my mom? My imagination struggled to lock down what happened. Each thought was leaving more questions than it answered.

When we visited Grandma and Grandpa, I never asked my mom if this was the house she grew up in. The house where Grandma pulled the kitchen knife? I was too afraid to imagine the scene, the wholeness of it all. The bright yellow laminate kitchen counters covering every inch of space. The nut-brown upper and lower cabinets with the pencil-thin black lines running down them like sad lines on a person's face. The gold handles, tarnished and worn from years of use.

Looking down and across—nothing but diamond vinyl with chestnut brown, decorated with a matrix of pale salmon-pink and yellow flowers pointing in the direction of Mom's old room. The burnt coffee smell that percolated and permeated for hours, that saturated into the wood.

I imagined when she pulled the knife out, the little wheels squeaked on the metal track as she opened the drawer. I wondered—do murderers shut the drawer or just let it hang open like it just happened? When you slowly opened the door and saw the drawer open, you would almost feel the warmth of the bodies just lying there.

.

*

Admission to University of Minnesota May 26, 1978 – June 27, 1978:

This ten-month-old girl was admitted for evaluation of poor weight gain and pneumonia. As you know, Tessa had ileal atresia and meconium peritonitis as a newborn. At that time, a sweat chloride was done, which was 37. She did not do well at home and was admitted to Mercy Hospital at one month of age for evaluation of failure to thrive. Her appetite had also decreased, and her intake had been severely restricted; patient's weight 4.78 kilograms (10.5 lbs.). Her white count 19,800.[4]

The diagnosis of cystic fibrosis is made on Tessa Weber based on primarily her sweat chloride results and also on her history and presenting condition of pneumonia and poor weight gain. Due to the nature of the disease, Tessa was discharged on the following medications: Aquasol vitamin A, 5000 units daily; Aquasol vitamin E, 50 units daily; Vi-Penta, 0.6 cc. daily; vitamin K, 5 mg. weekly; and Gentrisin suspension, 250 mg. three times daily. Tessa's parents have been supplied with a mist tent, water purifier, nebulizer, suction, and suction catheter. They have also been trained in performing bronchial drainage and clapping on Tessa. Dr. Warren Warwick plans to see Tessa in the Cystic Fibrosis Clinic in one month's time. Her diet on discharge was Pregestimil, 8 ounces five times daily, plus puree, and 1 1/2 packets of Cotazyme with each feeding. With her present therapy and dietary supplements, it is felt that Tessa's prognosis is good and that she can look forward to many years of a relatively normal life-style.[5]

---

[4] Third admission. University of Minnesota Twin Cities. The value of sweat chloride, 37. A normal value is less than 40. "She did not do well at home." Upon admission: 10lbs. 5 oz. WBC 19,800. Pg. 2: Sweat chloride at this admission 75 and 80, tested twice. "The diagnosis of cystic fibrosis is made on Tessa Weber based on primarily sweat chloride results and also on her history of presenting condition of pneumonia and poor weight gain. Tessa's prognosis is good and that she can look forward to many years of a relatively normal life-style [sic]."

[5] Image description: a photograph of a portion of Tessa's diagnostic report. It reads: The diagnosis of cystic fibrosis is made on Tessa Weber based on primarily her sweat chloride results and also on her history and presenting condition of pneumonia and poor weight gain. Due to the nature of the disease Tessa was discharged on the following medications: Aquesol vitamin A, 5,000 units daily; Aquesol vitamin E, 50 units daily; Vi-Fenta, 0.6 cc. daily; vitamin K, 5 mg. weekly; and Gentrisin

At birth, I was tested for cystic fibrosis (CF), but the result was negative. Cystic fibrosis is typically tested with what is known as a salt test. CF patients have higher salt content on the outside of their skin as well as other organs. If a newborn is suspected to have CF, a salt test is calculated. However, babies do not sweat very much, and a negative diagnosis was obtained. My salt content was 37, a normal value.

Normal white cell count is up to 10,000. If the white count is above 10,000, there is an infection in your body. My white count was mostly due to my pneumonia and lung infection. Above 18,000, the infection has made its way into the bloodstream. At nine months of age, I weighed 10.5 lbs.

Cystic fibrosis is a progressive, genetic disease that causes persistent lung infections and limits the ability to breathe over time. There is a salt and water imbalance in the lungs and sweat glands, and for some people with CF (CFers), the pancreas as well. Consequently, CF cells are "unable to move chloride, a component of salt, to the cell surface." Without chloride to attract water to the cell surface, thick and sticky mucus forms.[6]

When bacterium grows into CF lungs, CFers often do not have enough water to wash away the bacteria, unlike non-CFers. The bacterium stays, nests, and creates an infection, and then repeated infections. The bacteria destroy lung tissue over the years. The body tries to fight by releasing lymphocytes and macrophages, creating inflammation. Many CFers lose lung volume over time, over the years, and some patients need a lung transplant, or they die.

---

suspension, 150 mg. three times daily. Tessa's parents have been supplied with a mist tend, water purifier, nebulizer, suction, and suction catheter. They have also been trained in performing bronchial drainage and clamping Tessa. Dr. Warren Warwick plans to see Tessa in the Cystic Fibrosis Clinic in one month's time. Her diet on discharge is Progestimil, 8 ounces five times daily, plus purees, and 1½ packets of Cotazyne with each feeding. With her present therapy and dietary supplements, it is felt that Tessa's prognosis is good and that she can look forward to many years of a relatively normal life-style [sic].

[6] https://www.cff.org/intro-cf/about-cystic-fibrosis

I remember sitting on mom's lap; I was four years old. I watched her pick her hair. Remember when people used to *pick* their hair, like fluff it in that '80s dramatic way. Spritz it with hairspray afterward. She didn't do the fluff. She instead took the pointy ends of the pick and pushed them on her scalp and moved it back and forth slightly. Her scalp itched because she hadn't washed her hair in days. It had a shine of grease, like black oil.

Then she had a clip in her hair, one of those monstrous clips with long plastic teeth joined by a wire. You squeezed it, and the monster opened its large mouth to eat you. She bunched up her hair and pulled most of the hair to one side, sitting aloof on the top of her head, while she picked at the other side. Clip, swoosh, pick. This was when her depression deepened. Below the floor joists, below the cement basement floor, below the roots of the earth.

Sitting, with my legs stretched out across her lap, I stared at her white nightgown with pink flowers scattered, plotted evenly over the fabric. Her pink lace collar with a shaded ring of brown below it from days of wear, and watched her pick, pick, pick her hair. Clip, swoosh, pick.

"Are you going to wash your hair?" I asked. Her eyes shot at me. She put her pick down on the side table, picked me up readily, got up, and walked away. The bubble and the pick melded.

A coolness went up to my arms and down my legs. I stood there cold. My whole body clutched. A mistake. I miscalculated.

My mom repeatedly said, "I hate liars. Always tell the truth." The truth was she needed to wash her hair. Was the truth the mistake? No. Only upsetting my mom was the mistake.

*

Admission August 24, 1978 – September 2, 1978:

This is the second University of Minnesota admission for this one-year-old who was diagnosed as having cystic fibrosis. Her presenting problems were failure to thrive and persistent right upper lobe infiltrate.

Course in hospital: Problem #1: Nutrition. Tessa's admission weight was 6.0 kilograms (13.2 lbs.) approximately the same as on discharge two months ago, 5.98 kilograms. She initially took a large amount of Pregestimil without any problems, but then did have some episodes of vomiting requiring I.V. fluid supplemental and potassium supplementation. However, by the time of discharge, Tessa was tolerating all feedings well and her discharge was 6.5 kilograms.

Problem #2: Temperature spike. Tessa developed a temperature of 104 degrees on the second day of admission. Temperature now resolved. Tessa is therefore being discharged with a history of poor weight gain and feeding intolerance. This is felt to be possibly related to stress in the home, and this will be followed up by social work and social services.[7]

*

Question 5:

Me: *In one of my pictures, I flipped it over, and it says, 'Nurse.' What was the main purpose the nurse was appointed at home? How long did both*

---

[7] September 6, 1978:
ADM: 8/24/78
DIS: 9/2/78
Discharge Summary
Fourth admission, 2nd for University of Minnesota. Failure to thrive and persistent right upper lobe infiltrates. Decreased in food intake, 4 ounces max per feeding. Upon admission: 13 lbs. 2 oz. Just shy of 12 months and two weeks old with a weight gain of 6lbs. 1 oz.
Pg. 2: Temperature spike of 104. WBC 14,800. Bowel infection with lymphocytosis (immune system is working to fight infection). "Tessa is therefore being discharged with a history of poor weight gain and feeding intolerance. This is felt to be possibly related to stress in the home." A follow-up with social work and social services. Check up in two weeks.

of you have a nurse appointed to help you at home (i.e., one month or two months?) When was she appointed at home, i.e., how old was I and how many days a week?

Mom:

1st question: *To check your progress & my progress (dealing w/ everything). Eating was for sure a problem.*

2nd question: *One month to six weeks.*

3rd question: *Appointed—you were about eleven or twelve months old. One day a week.*

Question 6:

Me: *What did the nurse do?*

Mom: *Just to see if you were progressing. And how I was handling everything.*

Question 7:

Me: *What were the most difficult times to get through? When were both of you told about my life expectancy?*

Mom:

8   Image description: The handwritten response to question 7 from Tessa's mother. It reads:
1st question: Horrible first year of your life. Getting you diagnosed & then getting the doctors at the U (& nurses) to understand you wouldn't drink that awful, awful, Pregestimil (milk stuff).

My mom preferred to live in 'La, La, Land.' Choosing not to know the details in life, preferring the details in pretty things. She bought button-down silk blouses, plush fur coats, and black leather gloves. A diamond or two, perfume she dabbed gracefully on her wrists. The décor with porcelain figurines placed in every corner of the house. That eagle that could soar. "Don't you just love the bald eagle. It's so beautiful," she would say. Silk drapes, fluffed rugs, plentiful in number for rotation around the room and around the house. The need to be pristine. The couch one could not lay their head down on unless you set a towel underneath first. Take your shoes off at the door or prepare to be scorned. Wipe each drop of water around the sink, or else.

She adorned what she could, but by soaking in and soaking up all the 'bad words' in her life, my mom never allowed them to dry or to find their way out. When she met my dad, those words settled into their new home. A good man, but with a drinking problem.

I could say he just drank a lot, but that would be lying. Even at the age of seven, I knew my father was a drunk. I hung out with him in the garage while he drank. He was a woodworker by night and a machinist by day. He signed himself up to go into the Navy before the US Army took him by way of the draft. He took the skills he learned in the service and applied them to the private sector, building parts for ships. He had a motorcycle, and he smoked, but who didn't. Some evenings he drank one bottle after the next, pulling out a new bottle and popping off the cap on his workbench.

"Can you hand me a bottle?" He would ask. I took one and opened it. I felt like I was my dad's sidekick. Even if I didn't have the knack to pop it off yet, eventually I learned. Before passing it to my dad, I often put

---

2nd question: Nine months & finally diagnosed. & I believe the intern said: you'd live to seven, eight, or nine years of age. That was horrible & I never asked that question again. I really preferred to live in La, La Land. In other words, I wanted us as a family to live a normal life at home. I didn't want that negative stuff in our lives. Negativity breeds negativity! I really believe this.

my lips on it and blew, making a whistling noise. Every once in a while, I took a sip. I was curious about how it tasted. I handed it to him, and he sipped and slugged it back and put the bottle back empty. Twenty-four bottles in a case, and some nights he drank them all.

"You don't call yourself a drunk when you drink twenty-four bottles in a night?" My mom asked. I stood there and thought she had a point. My dad didn't always drink that much, but he enjoyed it when he could.

I passed him some beer; he showed me how to do fractions. He measured cuts of wood; one-fourth, one-half, three-fourths. How much was one-fourth and one-half when you added them together, three-fourths. He always had a pencil sitting behind his ear. While figuring, he slid his pencil out and jotted the number down. Sometimes he held the pencil in his mouth in mid-thought.

My mom only allowed my dad to smoke outside, and I hung out with him, despite my lungs. He tried to hold the cigarette up and away from me, saying, "You shouldn't be out here."

Even with his warning, I stayed. I liked watching him cut pieces of wood using his table saw. He slowed down his pace when my interest increased. Since my mom always had him working, the more time I had with my dad. He created and designed our two-story porch and our barn out back, yellow with brown trim and door. He finished the basement, took a wall down upstairs, redid the kitchen, stained, cut, and hammered new trim throughout the house. He built a whole new addition to the front of the house with the help of my cousins.

In my dad's free time, I nudged him to play HORSE or dribble the ball around in the back. He put in a basketball hoop for me. We shoved the metal stakes in for croquet, hammered, and aimed the green, red, blue balls all over the backyard. He gave me my own mitt to practice throwing the softball back and forth.

When he drank, and the more he drank, he began to mumble. "What did you say?" Mom asked.

"Ah, nothing," he scrunched his face, put the pencil back behind his ear, and said nothing more. The more my mom asked, nagged, the more he ignored her and tossed another beer back.

"Your father came at me," she said to Andrew and me. "You two probably were too young to remember. I had new clothes on. My pink blazer and skirt, matching with my new ruffle white and soft pink blouse." My mom took her hands and grabbed the invisible blazer lapels as if she still had it on. "I was going to a home interior show. All packed and ready. Your father didn't want me to go. He lifted his cup of coffee and threatened to throw it on me. I said, 'Don't you dare.'

"'Dare what?' He said.

"He had that look." My mom meant the look when he drinks too much. I knew that look. The whites of his eyes elongated where the circle of blood thickened, and his pupils enlarged and became pierced.

"He chased me. I ran downstairs and out into the front yard. God knows what our neighbors thought. There he was, chasing me in the front yard." The deep throttle started. "He-could-have-burned-me." The corners of her lips went from straight face to a forced frown. She cried and sobbed; tears streamed down her face.

When the tension between them about split, he pounded on the kitchen table with his two fists. He spit out words, clenching his jaw so tight neither my brother nor I could make the words.

"I dare you, Robert. I dare you," my mother said.

*

Question 8:

Me: *When I was 0-3 years old, how stable was my health? Did my pulmonary function tests (PFT, lung volume) and weight go up and down a lot?*

Mom:

1st question: *0-1 year, your health was horrible. One time I remember your father calling home & asking me: 'What was it like in hell today?' You were starving to death, Tessa. And we just didn't know what to do. 2-3 years – Great, because we got you eating.*

2nd question: *No, actually once we got you on track, you just kept on improving w/ Dr. Warwick & God's help, of course.*

*

"If I could, I would hit you so hard it would make your head spin, sending it flying across the room. You are lucky you're my kids," Mom said. I used to break this sentence down so many times. I knew she would hit us if she could, more than a hand. Then 'flying across the room.' There went my head. But then she said the 'lucky' part. That is what confused me the most. 'We aren't mean people.'

*

Admission September 15 – September 25, 1978:

This is Tessa's third UMH admission for this one year, one month old white female with cystic fibrosis. Since diagnosis, Tessa has been a management problem for parents; however, they have been able to succeed with her respiratory care and medications. She is a poor feeder and often vomits up. As feedings are scheduled one every four hours, this is becoming intolerable for parents. The child inconsistently fusses during meals and pushes the spoon away. She will sometimes eat for one parent and not the other, and often reverses her pattern. Occasionally she will eat for total strangers but not for parents. This has been quite a strain on the mother, who is spending eight to ten hours a day attempting to feed the child. It seems to mother that the child indulges in purposeful vomiting.

*

Question 9:

Me: *What things did Dr. Warwick say that ingrained in your memory, even possibly until this day?*

Mom:

No. 1 – We would have to be very strict, Like God. If we weren't you would basically not survive. Because, you wouldn't do everything to do w/ CF. Now, that was an awful lot of pressure to put on any parent. Perfection plus God. You know, Dr. Warwick— Expectations wow!

No. 2 – We as parents could do everything right & it still could turn out wrong. We were always trying so hard.

No. 3 – You were the most improved patient & I was the most improved mom. ☺

9

The thing is, my mom could only hold back for so long. In every conversation, in person, on the phone, or in writing, she was like a slow growing fire. Her once short and poignant answers grew in length, enhanced in volume, while her physical letters ballooned in size.

Question 10:

Me: *How many times was I approximately in the hospital (the University) and how long were the stays?*

Mom:

1ˢᵗ time: Collapsed lung & diagnosed CF. Stay: Two weeks? Not too sure.
2ⁿᵈ time: You wouldn't drink that Pregestimil (milk, yuck!) They sent us home w/ a syringe to force feed you. Every four hours was the feeding

---

9   Image description: Handwritten responses to question 9 from Tessa'smother. It reads:
No. 1 – We would have to be very strict, like God. If we weren't you would basically not survive. Because, you wouldn't do everything to do w/ CF. Now, that was an awful lot of pressure to put on any parent. Perfection. Plus God. You know, Dr. Warwick—
Expectations Wow!
No. 2 – We as parents could do everything right & it still could turn out wrong. We were always trying so hard.
No. 3 - You were the most improved patient & I was the most improved mom [smiley face]

schedule! It seemed to be inevitable – you threw up that milk a lot & then,

of course, started to drink all over again.

3rd time: Other side (I'm just so windy)

---

10 Image description: A handwritten note from Tessa's mother in response to question 10 that
reads:

In moments of quiet I have wondered, what forces—all the forces in her life compelled her to say, 'I just might throw you' out loud, to another adult. How or why could she leave her child, a sick child? She was not restrained. She could have visited me.

She absorbed other people's words, opinions, presumed judgements of her, which changed her course. The idea of one sour look, straight-lipped scorn; she couldn't take it. She reached her threshold.

Thinning out the thicket, there is a lot of space between the words 'crazy,' 'throw you,' 'starving,' 'not listening,' and 'go figure.' Space where lips held tight. Blows, tears, blubbery sorrows. I can see my mom wipe her face with her hand while holding the phone in her other. And then her repetitive phrase, 'we aren't mean people.' I don't think my mom was a mean person.

Broken. My mom was broken. She had unresolved trauma, and she struggled every day to manage her own emotions, the rumble that rolled around in her soul. She had no support from her parents, and she didn't know how to heal her broken parts.

She was always on trial. She was trying to prove she did her best and that she was a legitimately good mother, even with the rotation of the words 'management problems' written throughout my records. Dragging herself through and reliving her trauma each time.

Mom had a huge melt down. It was force feeding—throwing up—start again. The same drill again & again. They didn't care, Tessa. The yucky milk was supposed to be the best for digesting. They didn't listen, No! Until, I went crazy. I called Dr. Warwick & told him, I just might throw you, and, just maybe, they should put you in a home where you would eat & live. They blamed everything on my being a Nervous Nelly! Gee, I wonder why? Tessa you were always crying. You were starving. Dr. Warwick was such a sweetheart. He told me, they would keep you 'til I was comfortable taking you there. I didn't go to the hospital for about 5 days after you were admitted. Papa went every day. What a sweety-pie [smiley face]. Then one special day—good news finally— nurse Mary Jo Somebody (not McCracken) called & told me on the QT reading the charts and even the best baby nurse couldn't get you to eat that stuff. You went 8hrs without eating. She said, Carol come to the hospital. Tessa's eating mashed potatoes, spaghetti, etc. From then on you were on a roll. How they could think that you can force feed any child. But, I & Papa had to go crazy first Go figure, by the way, Papa reminded me, we had a bucket & mop at all times in our kitchen

Love you sweetheart [smiley face]

She went to counseling once and walked out, saying, "You don't know my life," to the counselor. The door slammed again. The counselor didn't know my mom's life; we didn't know her life firsthand either. She only showed us her life through her suffering. Then by making others suffer, that was her way of telling her story.

Diagnostic Laparoscopy

I. What will the surgeon find inside me?

- blood and muscle
- inflammation
- scar tissue (to be expected)
- scar tissue (that wasn't expected)
- a box of Kleenex
- maybe that tampon I still don't know if I lost on the dance floor
  or if it got sucked into the black hole behind my cervix seven years ago
  when I got too drunk at that lesbian music festival
- the black hole behind my cervix
- two cups of black tea
- ten thousand swallowed tongues
- a handwritten prescription for hysteria, carved into my endometrium
- the map and boots my uterus used to wander the hills of my body
- a steam-powered mechanical iron mouth that says *I'm sorry*
  and only that, over and over again
- the peas I shoved up my nose in kindergarten
- pain, 11
- an old stone wall creeping through my guts
- a bomb
- endometriosis?

II. What the surgeon thinks he will find inside me:

- endometriosis

III. What the surgeon finds inside me:

- endometriosis

Willy Conley

The Galvanic Skin Response Test

A bilingual memory in American Sign Language recollection and English expression

age 4
me in hospital
doctor electric wires
tape tape tape
face, arms, legs

long, long spaghetti wires
to machine
connect, connect, connect

earphones over-my-head
feel-same vise (twist, twist, twist)
pressure-lock

red button
doctor finger press
suddenly
electric shocks
like rug me walk walk
touch doorknob
lightning sssssizzle!

Me jump out
but doctor grabs me back
WHUMP! on seat
spaghetti wires everywhere

Then machine tongue out
long thin paper
blue lines
fast up-and-down-
up-and-down-up-and-down...

Doctor head nods
he pats my leg
then rip, rip, rip
off tape
legs, arms, face
my eyes water fill
thought he tore off
my skin

Chisom Okafor

synonyms for tachycardia

pebbles flung into the night
a shower of leaves
falling off their branches
in a day full of wind.
here, within my aloneness
i pull two bread slices
into a magnetic field
with avocado pear for
margarine,
i make a vegetable sandwich
out of the void
like a god
on his creation morning.
i want to pretend i'm not
at the edge of ruin,
i want to look towards
the rising sun
& say into its face:
may your money perish with you
for what is empathy
if not a further annihilation
of an already dead thing.
once in a telephone conversation my father lowered his voice
and asked:
have you had lunch, son?

which is to say,
have you had your first
heart attack?
which is why i don't reveal
the state of my heart
anymore
or you become enslaved
to a conquest of eyes
pleading to a false innocence
teary in their hypocrisy
(& to a shiver of voices
curious in pseudo pity).
there is a difference
between a racing heart
& one drowning from having
too many horse-races
for one lifetime.

Laura Mulqueen

Imaginal Exposure

"you will be asked to go over the traumatic event while saying it out loud, in the present tense"

When the therapist asks *Are you back here now?* you stare

Start at beginning, in medias res: You've already backed away once and now he stands—above   vision   tunnel   *Try putting feet to floor.*

Roots running downward, frantic,
    snaking through the ceilings

of caves, seeking counsel in well-posed
    questions. *Stay with it.* Stalactites: drop

after drop of water, calcified.
    It was a formative experience.

Transformed by pain as growth, or else try
    burning your mattress in the dead of night

while moonbeams pull light from wings
    of roaches slinking down brick like blood.

You're still there, breath stalled
    in diaphragm knocked out by his panting,

the moonlight obscured by fluorescence.
    In a clinic armchair you've unfolded

hands, uncrossed legs, they wring
    back reflexively, repetitively you almost

whisper the words pulled   *What are you*
    thinking now? Feeling now?

from behind eyelids where vision
    is lost to cavernous black,

the walls: distance measured
    in the pause between each echo.

    "It is important to remember that even if you feel temporarily more upset
    after some exposure sessions, especially the early ones...

When the therapist asks *Are you back here now?*   you stare

    ...this just means that you are beginning to emotionally
    process these   memories."

at the valley where your fingertips
    press into thighs.

Cristina Hartmann

Carnaval, Upstate

I ran home from the bus stop, the cold mineral air of winter filling my lungs. Laughter vibrated in my throat as I passed our neighbor's powder-blue house with Christmas lights sagging over their front windows. I almost slipped on a patch of slush before catching myself. I didn't care that it was February in Syracuse, the worst month of all with its dirty brown snow and dirty gray skies. None of that mattered because today was Carnaval.

Panting, I stopped outside of the screen door to what used to be my only home. There was so much to tell Mamãe and Papai. About the swimming pool and the library at my new residential school. About how Shannon was my best friend now. About how there was a Deaf world and how different it was. But not about Kyle or what I had said to Shannon. Those I would keep to myself.

I opened the door, and warmth covered my face as Mamãe smiled up at me. Her mouth shaped some words that escaped me. Before I could figure them out, she swept me into her arms.

I must've gotten worse at lip-reading. I kept thinking about what she said, like playing a videotape over and over in my head. Then I think I got it: "You're finally home! Tell us everything."

Papai's glasses bumped my head as he hugged us. I breathed in his smell of laundry detergent as their arms encircled me. I was home now. Papai looked the same with his big dorky glasses and the blue button-down shirts he bought in bulk from K-Mart. His chest rumbled like he was talking. Sometimes he forgot that I couldn't hear him.

I told them how much I missed them and how wonderful, yet strange, school was. They stared at me in that confused way they had when someone spoke English too fast. It's funny how much you forget when you go away. Here, I used English or my voice. ASL was for school. I arranged signs in a more English way, which felt slow and clumsy. That didn't work either, so I spoke, twisting my tongue and trying to breathe right. The words finally came, "I missed you." I forgot how hard using my voice was.

They understood and hugged me again.

I inhaled to say more, but Papai walked away before I could stop him. When he picked up the phone, I understood. I wished they would tell me about things like when the phone rings. Anger bubbled up in me. This never happened at school.

It took a while for Mamãe to fingerspell *Roberto*, her fingers tripping over one another. She wasn't practicing, which meant she would forget everything. I was about to scold her until I saw the dried blood around her nails. She was working extra hours, washing dishes and scrubbing floors—for Papai and me. It wasn't a good time to talk.

I wanted to tell her what it was like at my new school, Rochester School of the Deaf, where I started eighth grade this year. Everyone used my sign name, *M* at the corner of the mouth, instead of just calling me Marina like hearing people do. Everyone talked so much there, words flowing so fast that it made me dizzy. Sometimes I didn't know what to say, like with Kyle and Shannon, which is strange since I'm supposed to know how to talk to everyone there.

RSD was nothing like my old school where everyone was hearing, which was all right for a while. Some kids learned signs like "turtle" and "poop," good enough for us to talk a little and play games like Spit. That changed last year, though. My best friend Delia started saying that it was rude to point and make faces, but that's how sign language works. The other girls only talked about boys, usually forgetting to face me so I could lip-read, and kept laughing without telling me why.

I told Alice about this when she came for our weekly meetings. She was my teacher of the Deaf who knew about Deaf things, and the school administration said she would help me achieve my full potential—whatever that meant. After I talked about how Delia hurt my feelings, Alice looked sad. "She's hearing," she said. "It's hard for hearing people to understand what it's like having to try so hard to communicate." That was when she told me about RSD.

When I asked to go there, Mamãe cried, and Papai said that the education wasn't good. I told them that I wanted to be somewhere everyone understood each other. I don't know if that's what happened.

*

Carnaval was in the air. *Feijoada* bubbled on the stove, filling the basement with the smell of beans, onions, and meat. Bright reds and blues covered up the awful beige walls our landlord wouldn't let us paint. Carnaval was better than Christmases and birthdays because you celebrated surrounded by dancing. When I described this to Shannon, she said that the costumes sounded weird. Kyle laughed at the idea of clowns at my house, even though I had explained that it wasn't like American carnivals.

Carnaval means happiness and new beginnings. You dance when it's cold and gray outside. Everyone dresses up to welcome the spring together. Maybe it's different in Brazil since it's summer there when it's winter here.

Mamãe snatched a feather from Papai with that mad-annoyed look that she got when I forgot to take out the trash. Their mouths moved in that Portuguese way. Papai touched her cheek and said something that made her stop waving the feather. She didn't look happy, but she didn't look mad either. I wished I knew what he had said. I forgot most of my Portuguese after I got sick and went deaf when I was two. Teachers told my parents that they should only speak English with me. Something about how English and sign language were more important. So that's why they use only English with me even though they're lousy at it. Sometimes Mamãe speaks Portuguese by accident and cries when she realizes her mistake.

As she hung paper palm trees, Mamãe's hips swung like a pendulum, gentle and soothing. Papai bobbed his head in that dorky way of his. I was thinking about how silly they looked when I understood. Music was playing, too quiet for me to feel.

Before I could ask them to turn up the music, Mamãe's mouth outlined something like dress before sashaying down the hallway. Papai crouched by the big stereo, wires dangling from his mouth with a crumpled manual next to him. Even though he's good at science, Papai's no good with machines. He broke the furnace once, and we had to sleep in our parkas for a week. He seemed too busy to talk, so I followed Mamãe.

She sat behind a pastel-green sewing machine with pins sticking out from her mouth. She looked so peaceful that I didn't want to spoil it. She was making one of her creations, clothes that belonged in fancy stores with shiny floors.

She could be more than a housekeeper. I once found a photograph of her standing next to a tall blonde wearing a yellow dress that floated around her body like a cloud of daisies. It said, "Rio Fashion Week 1984" at the bottom, which was the year before I was born. When I asked her why she didn't go to New York to show her dresses, she looked sad and fingerspelled, "Can't. Love you both too much." Now she babysits and cleans "under the table" because Papai is here on a student visa.

She slid the fabric into the machine, her fingers so close to the needle that it looked like she'd hurt herself, but she didn't. Every stitch was perfect. A soft smile grew on her face that made her look younger and not so tired. When she looked up and saw me, the smile changed. I can't explain how, just that it did.

She snipped a thread, and the dress was done. She wriggled into it, and I gasped. It was one of her best. Reds and purples swirled around her hips and breasts, making her look curvier and taller. After I fastened the back, she twirled and her mouth moved, "You like?"

My fingers swept around my face: *beautiful*.

Her eyes lit up, and the soft smile returned. She remembered the sign. She pointed at the mirror, and her lips moved, "Same. We the same."

We looked more alike than I remembered with our thick black hair and lips that pouted without looking sad. Up close, I saw how different we were. Her lips bright with lipstick and eyelashes heavy with mascara, she was so dazzling that I almost didn't notice the wrinkles around her eyes. I looked plain with my face bare of color and jeans that sagged at the knees. She wore a gorgeous painting.

"I want to dance in a dress like yours," I said, the words thick in my mouth.

Her hand went to my cheek. "Later. Too young."

I scowled at my reflection. I hadn't been too young to have a boy slide a hand up my shirt last week.

When Kyle led me to an empty room after class, I thought he wanted to ask me about an essay on *Shiloh*. Instead, he asked if he could kiss me. After thinking about it, I said yes. I wanted to know what it was like.

It felt like an alien ship landing on my mouth that tasted like warm orange juice. I didn't like it at first, then I understood why all of the girls talked about kissing. It was like the heat from his mouth spread throughout my body, warming up all of me. That felt good, so good that I wanted more. So I let him lift up my shirt and put his mouth on my breasts.

The next morning, the other boys waggled their eyebrows as I walked by. The girls turned away, but I saw their hands twisting at their cheeks: *slut*. I never told anyone about the kiss, so Kyle must have.

Kyle wasn't popular just because he played basketball and looked like Leonardo DiCaprio, except with dark eyes and hair that's always in his eyes. He came from a Deaf family, which meant that his parents, grandparents, and even great-grandparents were all Deaf. His parents were important people. His dad taught at the university, and his mom did what they call advocacy work. Shannon said that this is the best kind of family because everyone understands each other.

*

I found Mamãe and Papai in the living room, arms wrapped around each other as they danced. The only time that Papai danced well was with Mamãe. Otherwise, he bobbed his head like a duck. She said that it was because he was from São Paulo. "They too serious. We Rio people know how to have fun!" They must've forgotten I was there because they looked like they would kiss, so I left. It never seemed like the right time to talk to them.

Half of the living room was now in my bedroom. A couch leaned against the wall, surrounded by boxes full of Papai's textbooks. Mamãe's mannequins blocked the way to my bed. I missed my bed at school where Shannon and I talked after lights out using a flashlight.

When I first arrived at school, Shannon grabbed my hand and showed me around. Even though she looks like a popular girl with the way she walks with her back straight and head thrown back, she's not stuck-up. She showed me the classrooms, told me which teachers would let you hand in homework late like Mr. Titus and who wouldn't like Ms. Rausch, and to say "I'm Deaf, too" if I saw another Deaf person. We talked about who was cute, like Kyle, and who wasn't, like Barry. When she invited me to her home three weeks ago, I said yes.

She lived in a big house in Buffalo with four bedrooms, a silvery kitchen, and a finished basement with a big TV. Shannon's mom was really pretty in that magazine kind of way where she wore clothes with boring colors like gray or taupe but somehow looked beautiful. When she brought us hot chocolate, she moved her mouth in that careful way people use with Deaf people, which made Shannon embarrassed for some reason. Her mom was good at it, though, and didn't speak too slowly or make weird faces. That's why I understood her at dinner.

Shannon was slouching at the dinner table when her mom said, "Shannon, have you been practicing?" with a teacher-type of look, "It's important to keep up your articulation." Shannon's face reddened and she yelled, "I told you! No more!" with her hands flying. She ran off and slammed the door so hard the floor shook.

Her mom turned to me with that confused expression that you see on foreigners, which looked all wrong on her face. I think she wanted to ask what Shannon said because her fingers twitched like she wanted to sign but she picked up the dirty plates instead. Before she walked away, I saw tears in her eyes.

I had never seen Shannon so upset before. Her hand almost hit the lamp as she told me about the speech lessons. "My mom says I'm not trying hard enough. I tried so hard! I'm just not good at it." She opened and closed her mouth in a way that made speaking look ridiculous and paused like she was thinking hard. "She's not really my family. You and I are a real family. We understand each other."

Her hands drew a circle in the air between us, like we belonged together. I thought of how much I liked talking to her and the other kids at school. They didn't say things like "Never mind," or "It's not important." My hands could move as fast as my thoughts, and their eyes never got that confused look. I hugged Shannon and told her we were a family.

When we went to sleep, I thought of Mamãe and Papai, their eyes full of hurt. If I were part of the Deaf family, how could I still be part of theirs? I lay awake, wondering how to fit two circles together.

Now, Shannon was mad at me. When I said that I wanted to tell off Kyle for blabbing, she shook her head. "You have a chance to get the perfect family, so don't screw it up!" she said. She didn't hug me goodbye before I left, and I didn't know what to say to either one of them.

*

I was flipping through one of Papai's textbooks about something called quantum mechanics when I felt the vibrations—the bed shaking to the beat of samba drums. Carnaval was finally here! I flung open the door, and the vibrations hit me in the chest. People had their hands in the air, swaying to the music that pounded throughout my body. Roberto waved at me from the corner, a big smile on his face.

I've always thought Roberto was good-looking, maybe even better looking than Kyle. He's skinny with curly black hair tied back in a ponytail, which doesn't make him look like a girl at all. He smiles at you like he wants to be your friend. Kyle smiles like he has lots of friends already.

"You're back! How's school?" he signed.

I pressed my cheek against his chest and inhaled his smell—Pert shampoo mixed with something spicy. I forgot for a moment that I had been away.

Roberto moved in upstairs when he was a graduate student and never left, even though he's a teacher now. He watched me whenever my parents had to work, which was a lot. He learned to talk with me, and now he can sign really well for a hearing person. He said it was because he plays guitar. I think it's something else.

"School's good," I said, trying not to think about the boys' waggling eyebrows.

"You're so far away. It's too quiet here now."

I thought about telling him everything. About how the other kids asked me if my family sold drugs. About what happened with Shannon. About how everyone had changed my sign name to *slut*. About how I felt different from the other kids even though we're all Deaf. But I couldn't.

When I was little, I imagined Roberto and me living upstairs and my parents living downstairs. We would have Carnaval parties every year with him translating for all of us. It would be perfect, and if I told him, it would ruin everything. I didn't know why, just that it would.

"Are you enjoying the party?" I asked instead.

A dimple appeared in his left cheek. "It reminds me of the discotheques in Mexico City." He gyrated like John Travolta, making me giggle.

His eyes got serious. His hands moved—"Tell me more about school"— until he caught sight of a blonde wearing a skirt too short for Syracuse winters. He promised to talk later and went to the blonde. She kept flipping her hair, which made her look like she had a neck problem. Roberto must've liked it, though, since they went upstairs together. Maybe she was his girlfriend, and he hadn't told me.

Bodies and colors swirled around me as people talked, laughed, and danced. Lips shaped into different languages. Portuguese had more lip-puckering and moved faster. English was slower, with the mouth opening wider. Spanish was somewhere in between. No matter how hard I tried, the words stayed out of my reach.

I bumped against a table full of *caipirinhas*. Papai likes to drink them and say, "Only real Brazilians drink these. Americans keep their watery beers and snobby wines." His eyes always glazed over, and he acted like he didn't have to worry about money or his dissertation.

I stared into the cup, wondering what it tasted like. Everyone said that drinking was bad. Teachers. Roberto. Mamãe and Papai. The word *no* appeared in my mind, the oval mouth-shape, the fingers clamping together. I wanted to tell everyone *no*. No to Mamãe and Papai for not understanding me. No to Kyle for blabbing. No to the name-calling at school. No to Roberto for not telling me about his girlfriend. No, no, no!

The drink burned all the way down. How could Papai like something so awful? I must've missed something, so I drank another and another. It was like kissing. The more I tried it, the more I liked it. The sweet and tart blended into something so delicious that nothing else mattered.

Nobody noticed. Everyone kept dancing, dancing, dancing.

The floor turned wobbly like jelly. A red feather bounced in the air, so beautiful, and a pleasant heaviness weighed down my limbs. Somehow the colors, the movements, everything around me, had become more vivid, more real.

BOOM, badum—badum—tish. BOOM, badum—badum—tish.

The beat flowed through my body, the drums pounding as I swayed, swayed. Everyone was twisting and turning, the colors of their masks blurring together. It felt like we were living inside one of Mamãe's dresses with colors floating all around us.

BOOM, badum—badum—tish. BOOM, badum—badum—tish.

Expressions of ecstasy surrounded me as everyone lost themselves in the dance. Oh, I wanted to reach out and touch their happiness, or maybe I could. I didn't just want to watch, not anymore.

Cuica—cuica—BRRRUUUU—UUM! BOOM, badum—badum—tish. BOOM, badum—badum—tish.

I wanted to dance. Why hadn't I thought of this before? It was so obvious! The drums inside me had to escape, I needed to go out there and dance, dance, dance.

Hot, sweaty bodies pressed against me. I raised my arms and waited for the dance to come. Nothing happened...my body wouldn't move... a man looked angry when I stepped on his foot...I'm sorry...I tried to follow everyone else...I tried harder...Stiff limbs...Nothing was working!

Tears stung the back of my eyes. I turned and saw her.

Mamãe was dancing on top of a table, her hips whirling in figure-eights. The lines of her dress swirled together into whirlpools of color. Oh! So beautiful. A smile lifted her mouth as she reached up. Oh! The picture was interrupted when Papai brought her down to dance with him. They swayed together in perfect harmony.

The table stood empty, looking sad. Mouths opened in "Dance! Dance!" I took an outstretched hand and jumped onto the table. Everything started to spin, and I squeezed my eyes shut. The music felt sharper, clearer here. *Cuica—cuica—BRRRUUUU.* My body loosened, moving to the beat pulsing upward. *Badum—badum—BOOM.* Yes, yes, yes! Sway, lift, shimmy, twirl. I was dancing! Dancing, dancing, dancing! *Rum—brum—BRRRRUUUUU—UUM!*

Laughter burst out of me. The dance flowed through me, bringing with it everyone's joy. I belonged here. Twirling, twirling, twirling.

Something grabbed me, and I almost fell off the table.

Papai's hand was on my arm—why?—and he swept me off the table. His hand kept me in place as Mamãe's worried face appeared. Her lips moved in meaningless shapes, nonsense, gibberish. I shook my head. What did she say? What was happening?

Hands—theirs? someone else's?—pushed and pulled at me. Papai's glasses flashed the reflection of Carnaval's colors. Everything went double, two of Papai and Mamãe, four anxious faces, six mouths flapping in nonsensical shapes. What? Why? The harder I tried to catch the words, the more they slipped away. I was sick of always chasing the mouth-shapes, trying so hard to understand, of not being understood. Enough!

My fingers moved—flying, swooping, dancing—as my words flowed in torrents. Why don't you know my language? Don't you know what that means? It means that you don't know the Deaf world, you can't understand me, and if you don't understand who I am, how can you love me? How can we be a real family? My hands danced in the air, all of my thoughts unleashed, free of slow movements and cramped tongues. Don't you understand, Mamãe and Papai? Don't you want to be my family?

Someone jostled me, breaking the circle I was drawing in the air. Papai looked like someone had punched him. Mamãe put her face into her hands, her shoulders shaking like she was crying. They stayed there, looking small and broken. Even if they didn't understand the words, they felt their force.

Everyone kept dancing around us, making me dizzy and queasy. My stomach cramped as I circled my fist on my chest—I'm sorry—and ran, ran to the bathroom. I was going to be sick.

The white bottom of the toilet bowl gleamed as Mamãe held my hair back. My stomach clenched, and everything came up. My mouth burned afterward. Papai's arm felt warm around my shoulder as I fell into their bed.

*

I woke up with a dry mouth and a throbbing headache. Mamãe was sitting by me with a glass of water and an aspirin, her face scrubbed clean. She looked younger, more like me. I gulped down the water, the most refreshing thing I had ever tasted. She started to talk, her hands too slow for her mouth. I was too young to drink. Carnaval wasn't an excuse to misbehave. I had to clean up the mess as punishment. That was what she said, more or less.

She pressed her cool hand to my forehead, her eyes full of melancholy as if she wished for something she could never have. Her lips moved in that Portuguese way, and I caught a word, *amor*, love. The strange expression vanished, and her palms came together, "Clean up now!"

My head pounded as I went into the living room. It was a mess. Empty paper plates and cups were everywhere, even on the new stereo, which had a big brown puddle on top. I hoped Papai hadn't seen that yet. My foot caught onto some lumps in the carpet. Someone had stepped on some *pão de queijo* and smashed it deep into the fibers.

I felt footsteps behind me and turned to see Roberto. "Crazy Carnaval this year, uh?" he said after hugging me. "Sorry that I missed your dance show."

My blush made him laugh.

"We all need a release sometimes. Otherwise, you're too bottled up to think straight. Things look better afterward," he said before grabbing an overflowing trash bag and heading outside.

Papai came to kiss my forehead. His eyes had the same sadness as Mamãe's had. Maybe they understood what I had told them yesterday—not everything, but enough. And they still loved me.

The vacuum rumbled as I passed it over shreds of feathers and fallen confetti. As I cleaned, my thoughts untangled, and I finally knew what to say. To Kyle, I would say that it doesn't matter that he's popular because I don't kiss blabbermouths. To Shannon, I would explain that I don't need perfect families, just a real friend. That made me feel better, ready to go back.

I turned off the vacuum when it reached two paper plates on the carpet, stacked like a Venn diagram. I picked them up and tried to mash them together, but they crumpled without merging. I stared down at the crushed circles that would never become one and put one on top of the other. Maybe this was just how things were. Two circles, two families, and two lives. Two was more than one, and maybe that wasn't so bad.

Rob Colgate

Precocious

Skhizein — to split — phrēn — the mind — I'll cry — if they split us — apart.

You were drawn by hands that wanted to throttle your slippery neck,
Madness.
  Floated in an ocean that once marked
    the edge of the world,
      trod with the cartographer's
    monsters.
You survived when the hands thought
  you were a lake, then a fate, then a line unstraight
    cut through a history of cut brains,
  frontal lobe like feathers of a bird.
 How you flew
  when the hands tried to crush you like eggshells.
You were a dog they called a fox
  until your red sullied their homes—
    then you were a wolf, rabid fear at night.
 Get out of this house, before the hands
    name you; *dementia praecox*, hebephrenia,
    insanity.
Run, Madness— we need you
  to survive until someone names you with love.
    Don't leave me. I need you
      to survive.
You must survive being *wrecked*
  on the cliffs of puberty. Learn to swim.
 Learn to drown in just the right way
  so that you can do it over and over again.

You must climb out of the volcano
     and begin your *lifelong smoldering, your whole body metabolizing*
                              in a decisive cascade.
          We need you to learn to drink lava
                    more than once.
     Do you realize that your form need not be solid, that you can melt to hide?
     How weak are you, truly, how defective?
                         Did you defect from Illenau?
          Did the hands call you stuporous when you were merely precocious?
They navigate a hook around my eye
     to pull you out. They do not ask
                    where you want to go, how it might look there
     — a book of poems — a sutured home —
                              somewhere you would make
                              sense.
You would make nonsense into a sky
     glowing with planets in perfect orbit, each filled with oceans
          of mappable currents, if only the hands unhooked you
                              into the universe you wanted.
But they did not. They did not hear your plea or even consider
                    that you might have one.
     No, Madness, they took my mind and split it,
                    thalamus as tall grasses wilting, and now
when I run through the meadow
     I don't hear your voice,
                    so I lay in the dirt and my temperament slips
                         out of my mouth.
Do you remember when the hands said they had discovered you,
     how you told them that you hadn't been hiding
                    as they bored a hole in the osseous border of your
                    native land.

Come home to me now.

You are the self and I am the body. Let us smother each other.

Get in bed. In my head

you are my head and we sleep like an insulin

coma.

When they uncover my body

your arm and mine will be twisted together

reaching through the socket of my skull.

Sarah Allen

Turner Syndrome

We are nothing-missing
as a pelican's gular,
whole as chicken scratch.
Behold the short beaks

for gathering preciousness.
The Flanders fields of infertile nests

are not new, only the someones
who do the collecting.
The rarities who hatch
in treasure bowers

of the flightless.
Uses for broken boughs:

winter, feathers that are red,
genetic breadcrumbs scattered toward
home, incubators for surplus oxygen
and the milk of cut Calotropis.

The cradle is falling
and the crowned lapwing

nests on the ground.

Elizabeth Meade

When I Stutter

Sometimes, m's elongate,
grow long tongues to taste the last bit
of breath my body has to offer.

Sometimes, i's echo
like the harsh cries of a seagull,
try to fly far away from the nest of my mouth
only to circle the ocean of my uncompleted sentence.

Sometimes, my breath becomes caught
in the chamber of my throat, my head cocked back
until the word — at last — launches out of my mouth like a bullet.
Or a punch.

(Sometimes, my soft, raspy voice
provides no balm to soothe the ear.)

Sometimes, I remember Daddy said my voice
sounds like Mommy's. I rejoice then, as syllables
trip over one another like eager children
rushing toward the playground
with all the freedom her voice no longer has.

All that remains is the deep ache in my throat,
vocal cords like mud stomped flat
under the feet of my rowdy utterances.

Natalie E. Illum

My Mother's Prayer

My mother has one wish for me,
one daily mantra like *Good Morning,*
she calls to me over long distances.
Don't Fall. Try not to fall down.

OK. I promise. As though language mitigates
condition, as though my lack of balance
was semantics. So, I put down the phone.

Inside my head is a trip wire,
a stuttering endgame,
a wild gesturing

of genetics and alchemy. The equation of movement
sounds like static. A spastic afterthought of normal

encased in blue. I move forward through mud.

I go down and pick up the metaphor for pain
I call the bruising Persimmon. I hold lightening
in my synapses. I cushion the need for gravity.

Falling is like flying and the impact is not

death. I expect an easy shattering except
I get up. I haul muscle and torn

flesh into an approximation
of walking, a simulation of standing.
A promise I broke to my mother,

who swears every time I crash and cold sweat
threaten to break into my own skin. Every time
I grow bruises like purple and yellow crocuses
dying on my skin. She knows I have fallen
and prays for me.

Undertow

There is no body to bury, but then, there isn't much of a beach left, either. At low tide, after the water recedes from the road on the other side of the pylons, a strip of sand, logs, seaweed, and trash sits trying to remember itself. I suggested we wait for another hour before starting the ceremony to give the scavengers time to pass by. Some people don't like them—think of them as ghoulish or opportunistic. They pick through the debris, cleaning it from where it washes ashore, sorting, repurposing, and recycling. To me, they are custodians. Their hunched backs and punctuated muttering hold a disorganized kind of beauty. But I didn't think my family would appreciate their presence at Grams' memorial.

*

When I was twelve, my grandmother retired from teaching, left my grandfather, and moved to the west coast where she became a prolific ceramic artist with a side hustle as a certified whale detangler. She used her share of the divorce money to buy a house with Janet and her wife Emika. Grams and Janet had been best friends since university and for a hot minute the whole family thought for sure Grams would come out, but as it happened, she had only ever been a closeted hippy.

I was fourteen by the time Mom and I went for our first visit. I understood I was a queer girl by then and spending two weeks inside that house did me some very real good. I would sit entranced at the parties, beguiled at the breakfast table. I'm not the best at picking up on social cues or navigating casual conversations, but during that visit it was fairly easy to hide behind a label of shy. Floating in a swirling eddy of adults, I became more myself through silent shimmering osmosis. Grams, meanwhile, was full of stories of her work detangling whales. I begged to go out on a call, but neither she nor my mother was on board with that idea. I satisfied myself with sitting in Grams' studio, coated in drying clay like a second skin, lulled by the spinning of the wheel, the morphing shape of a vessel, and the sound of her voice.

*

"Mads, have you heard from your Grams?" Janet's usually mellow alto voice was tight and scratchy with fear. It clutched at my stomach, the muscles in my jaw tightening instinctively. That's how I found out she was missing. Although missing isn't exactly the word for it. I knew where she was; that is, I knew where she had gone. Everyone threw themselves into high gear looking for her. The authorities were notified, members of the whale detangling team that were still around headed out to help, the Coast Guard ran a search grid. Hazardous conditions complicated the operation. I spent most of my time communicating with my family. I could smell my anger, like diesel fumes and salt water, burning my nose. I wasn't angry that she did it, only that she hadn't said goodbye. Just before they found the dinghy, I realized she'd been saying goodbye for months.

*

When I was seventeen, I asked if I could stay with Grams and her friends for the summer, bring my drone, and record detangling missions. I got a job at an artisanal bakery near the beach. I liked it. It could get unbelievably hot in the kitchen, but the work was physical and satisfying, and there were days when I needed that.

Seven calls for whales in distress came in that season; I was able to go out for five of them. The first was a grey whale, probably an adolescent, whose tail was tangled in a sunken fishing line. It had likely been there for weeks, tethered to the ocean floor by tentacles of human industry. I flew the drone overhead, listening to the leader call out instructions and warnings.

"That's a distress blow," she shouted, "Careful now!"

The whale made deep groaning noises that reverberated inside my rib cage and sunk into my stomach like sharp rocks. I had trouble keeping the drone steady as my hands began to shake. The job was done with no injuries to anyone except the whale, who swam off in grace-filled exhaustion, deep gashes at the base of its fluke. I crumpled into the boat, feeling grateful for the vibration of the dinghy that carried us home. It covered my tremors.

Each time I went out, I felt my world focusing into small urgent pieces. The way the boat moved, the tension in the tangled lines and the muscles of the crew, the skin of the whale and the surface of the ocean. There was no room to feel anything during a call, but afterwards there was nothing but space. Space that filled with swelling, flowing emotion.

After the third disentanglement, I wandered down to the beach and sat on one of the big lumpy logs that littered the sand like cadavers. I was too full. There was nowhere left to put my feelings. Grams came with a hot chocolate protein drink in a large travel mug of her own making, decorated in shadows and smudges that resembled whales swimming in the dark of the ocean, if you knew how to look. She handed me the mug, sat for a long time in silence, then asked simply, "How's your heart?"

I started bawling. Deep, ugly, messy sobs. I wasn't so excited about going out in the boat after that. It was sombre work. It was humbling and shaming, and taking it seriously was quite literally the least I could do. I used every spare minute to edit footage and research whale entanglement and ship strikes. During the day, my mind swam with facts. At night, I dreamt in shifting shades of blue, my body moving amongst dark gentle shapes.

*

On the remains of the beach, we form a somewhat battered-looking crescent around a small portable fire pit. My parents and sister, uncle, aunt, and three cousins are there, as well as members of the whale rescue crew and a few friends. A bigger ceremony was held earlier at the hotel; this one is for family and close community members only. Janet suggested it based on something we organized for Emika's funeral a few years ago. The idea is simple: Because there was no body to honour, we would each burn something that personified Grams. It could be something that had belonged to her or something we had created—as long as it bound us together and it would burn. We take turns feeding the fire with letters, photos, and scraps of fabric. Among other things, I burn what is left of a loaf of sunflower seed banana bread after we pass it around, tearing off small portions for ourselves. It was the first recipe she taught me, the one we always went back to. When we're done, we add clay and paint pigment from Grams' workshop to smother the fire.

While the embers cool and the people who loved Grams most in the world shuffle, murmur, and wipe away tears on what was left of her favourite beach, I look out at the ocean and the sky. How is it possible that life has continued? Too much has disappeared and a hole too big to fill has been left behind. Surely things must fall apart. Waves roll, clouds move, but the pattern can't possibly hold, can it?

*

After that first summer, I went home to finish high school. I felt out of place in a way that finally made sense to me. I was on the wrong side of the mountains, the wind that greeted me was thin and tasteless. By Christmas that year, I stopped dreaming in blue and knew I had to get back.

I started the certification process to become a whale detangler, moved out to the coast as soon as I finished exams, and picked up my job at the bakery. I went out with the team whenever I could. Out there, I felt like I was doing something real, something that mattered.

Grams and I changed and shifted together; outlined in salt, tied to the same purpose. Her body stayed strong, but there were days when joints ached and muscles became too tender. There were times when I felt like I drew my growing strength from her and, as the years stretched, that flow of support and energy reversed. But when the real changes began, neither of us were sure where to look for help. I was a mission leader by then, but it's not like that made any difference. Eventually, we stopped going out at all.

*

The search only took three days. Grams had arranged to take one of the team dinghies out of storage, filled the tank, and headed out into the open ocean. The boat was found, but she had disappeared. The night of the memorial, in blue-on-blue shadow, I dreamt of the shape of my grandmother tangled in a fishing line, tethered to the bottom of the ocean. With hands I couldn't see, she and I worked together to release her, and she glided off into the dark, deep, bluer blue.

Lately, I walk around with a distressed moaning rattling my chest from the inside. I can't find a way to let it out. The other day a woman approached me as I was fixing the chain on my bike. I had tried to glance at her casually, but I probably got that wrong because looking at her, for the first time in a long time, I felt something pleasant and hopeful. She was all sensuality and sunshine wrapped in a sarong and wearing minimalist sandals made of thin rope and a simple flat sole. Her skin glowed and her hair fell in impossible honeyed-dark curls. As she came over to me, I was sharply aware of my beach butch self. My simple cropped haircut and practical workwear; my arm and hand muscles developed from years of kneading, my legs strong from cycling everywhere—with or without a carriage full of baked goods. I knew I smelled like the bakery. I have flour permanently hidden in the creases of my skin, caked beneath my fingernails and lightly dusting the inside of my lungs.

I became hyper-focused on the links in the chain, fumbling with the rollers and the teeth on the ring whenever I couldn't quite cope with the conversation. I do this thing a friend once called sideways flirting, where I aim my attention at something besides the person I'm interested in. I never really understand if it's working, but she seemed interested. Eventually she asked me, "So what do you do?"

I could have talked about the bakery, but instead I said, "I used to detangle whales."

"Oh," she paused, "Aren't the whales all gone?"

"Yes," I answered simply, staring at a smear of grease on my right index finger.

"So what do you do now?"

Her beauty faded for me then, diluted by my sorrow.

*

The whales began disappearing seven years ago. All of them. From everywhere. Sometimes group beachings would occur and despite all efforts they would die en masse, the final sighs of the whales knotted together with the cries of the humans who were trying to help them. At other times, multiple bodies would be sighted floating together. It was all gruesome and horrible, but for us, those were the worst: our work as detanglers having been transformed into body collectors. The scientists would arrive with bowed heads and heavy shoulders to perform necropsies as quickly as possible. There were vigils and marches. People wore t-shirts that read "Bring Out Your Dead" printed in wave-like text. Theories were floated, but nothing was ever definitively proven. It took a little more than four years for the last of the whales to disappear and another three before the scientific community came to a consensus: They were gone.

About a month after the announcement, after mention of it and the extinction had drained from the daily news coverage, Grams went out in the dinghy and disappeared. I knew exactly why she did it. I fought the urge myself. To be honest, I couldn't figure out how any of us were still alive. There were unavoidable disruptions. Of course there were. But maybe we were sinking too slowly to notice what was really happening.

*

Today I'm taking a dinghy to one of the islands uninhabited by humans. The oceans have finally begun to change and along with them the air, the soil, and the balance of all things. We are, after all, beginning to reckon with the consequences. Dead whale bodies used to be towed to these islands for examination. I know because I used to help tow them. The beaches are all submerged now under the rising water, but the bodies are still there. The ocean protects their story, inscribed in the sand by bones. I position the dinghy above them and lay down, my heart percussing against my ribs. It is the only song I have to offer, so I send it through the bottom of the boat, into the blue. And I wait. Empty, open for a song that will never be heard again.

Duane L. Herrmann

At Sixteen

The spring before his father died
was a hard year:
chronic social reject,
with raging hormones,
and home life
tortured as ever –
slipped off the edge
into free-fall.
Only tenuous connection
to this world:
walls no longer solid,
and they moved!
Colors took shape
and life of their own.
He struggled to see and walk.
Embracing trees
whispered him back
to this world.

C.M. Crockford

Isle

shoe bursts the old mayo pack
half-crumpled on a hot street

white stains brownstone brick
hollow shell left behind

wondering when it joins its brother garbage
in some godforsaken sea

when it becomes legion with leagues of plastic
this throne of litter this putrid isle

detritus of a thousand barren cities
who only grow who cannot die

expanding further outward further

until nothing on Earth breathes

but such are dreams of all trash
abandoned to the cracks
of a Philadelphia sidewalk

Teresa Milbrodt

You May Mistake This for A Love Story

His small office is attached to the main one but the door is often closed, so I see him mostly at the copy machine. He does not wear ties or use too much aftershave, suggesting he is unpretentious and honest. We make jokes about our cats. We both like cats.

This is a good sign, the first one. There will be more, and then we will date, and get engaged, and be married for nineteen years, and then we will get a divorce, mostly amicable, no lawyers, just threats of hiring them, a civility similar to the end of my first marriage.

I am taking notes on what will be our relationship, writing them on a pad at my desk in shorthand since no one else in the office can read it, and because I want to test my vision. I can see everything quite clearly, but my memory isn't as good as my sight. Thus, the notes.

*

This is what people used to believe: when you were deprived of one sense, the others would become keener. That was the world of a too-cruel and too-just god (don't think too deeply about it), one who'd smite you in a second or gift you with extraordinary abilities. My right eye has been blind since birth, so it has been blessed for an equally long period of time. It is the eye that Dalí would have loved. Malleable. Mutable. It can see anything but mostly the future, an invisible stick-on eye in the middle of my back, my forehead, my knee, under my left breast, over my heart. It is where it needs to be. While my left eye must squint to read the fine print, the right sees at a glance that the kid asking for a late pass

104

was making out with his girlfriend in the back of his mom's car during second period. Eye omnipotent. I give him the pass. Sometimes I am kind, even to liars. My right eye sees what it should and what it should not, playing on a separate screen in my mind. Actually, it isn't like that exactly, but the analogy might help you understand.

*

He's the assistant athletic director at the high school, almost like the assistant principal in that he works on schedules, charts grades, and yells at members of the football/basketball/wrestling teams if they're failing classes. He does not need a tie or aftershave to be taken seriously. I'm the administrative assistant, meaning I answer the phone, soothe irate parents, write hall passes, separate the honestly tardy from those who were smoking under the bleachers between classes, and generally serve as an all-knowing oracle and keeper of institutional information. In the future people will find it funny that he and I fell in love, but it is the classic myth. Jock dates nerd girl. Apollo chasing Cassandra. Think about it a moment and you'll see it's obvious.

*

My eye allows me to see love like a landscape. I take notes when no one is needfully standing beside my desk. The librarian will have an affair with the biology teacher—nice fellow, no kids, broke up with longtime girlfriend two and a half years ago, does laundry on Saturdays, plays guitar passably well, makes good stir-fry. The affair will last six months, just dinner and movies and sex at his apartment, then he'll move to a different school district in another state because the job pays more. They will both mourn. She'll feel betrayed but shoved by invisible hands to go to marriage counseling. Her husband will never know what happened. She'll think of him as sweet and oblivious. He'll wonder why she's suddenly more creative in the bedroom. (My eye squints to give them privacy.) This is as happy an ending as anyone can expect, and better than most.

*

You'd say I'm a liar, and I am, but listen to this: I knew I would marry my first husband then divorce him fourteen years, eight months, and six days later, a month before I turned thirty-nine. All our friends thought the split was too amicable, which may or may not have been true, but they hadn't seen what I had, the slow replacement of our cells over time, the crinkles at the sides of our eyes at different jokes, the changing tilt of our heads when we'd nod at each other after work, the shifting weight of a kiss on the lips, how it slid over months to a kiss on the cheek.

*

People shape you. You shape people. This is part of love. Because of my first husband, I eat a peppermint when I'm feeling stressed, make eye contact when I say hello, and know the biographies of three comic book superheroes. Because of me, he makes lists, doesn't feel offended when a woman holds the door, and knows the lyrics to '80s pop songs. There are words/images/notes we can't read/see/hear without thinking of each other. Everyone is an unwitting Pygmalion and a block of marble, the chisel and the shaking hand.

*

This will be the story of my third date with the athletic director: Going out for pizza, we both try to pay. He wants to be traditional. I have money, dammit, and he paid for the first two dates. We decide to take turns. This agreement will lounge in a corner of our minds even when we are married, even when we divorce. He cooks, I do dishes. He cleans the bathroom, I vacuum the cat hair (and cat hair and cat hair). We alternate weeks for grocery shopping and laundry. He does not expect me to iron his clothing, but he is not the sort of person who wears ties, so I assumed that courtesy. We devote equal attention, treats, and catnip toys to the felines we bring into the marriage and those that come after. It is our slavish attention to the illusion of fairness, the cooperation we strive for and almost never achieve, perfecting the drive for perfection.

*

My eye, an unwilling voyeur, is stuck to the back of my elbow in the lunch line when I buy bottled water and a turkey sandwich, seeing the high school cafeteria in all its beauty and drama, gossip hanging in the air like violet clouds. Remember, Romeo and Juliet were teenagers. Nobody understands that better than someone who works with high school students.

Yes, sometimes I want to rest my eye, close it, stick it in a mug with my pens, but it's always open. I wish I could be like the Graeae—you probably don't remember them, so I'll explain the story, how those three gray sisters shared one tooth and eye and fought over them constantly in a small, dank cave where I doubt there was much of anything to see.

But what a blessing, I think, to be occasionally blank, devoid of visions.

*

This is another myth few people know, how Medusa was a beautiful woman who made love to Poseidon in Athena's temple. The goddess was pissed—you never know what people will do when you're not home—so she changed Medusa into the snake-haired woman who turned soldiers to statues. Sad, I think, how we focus only on the end of the story, skip the part about making love and go directly to stone. How like and unlike humans.

*

The athletic director had two girlfriends before me, serious ones, neither of whom he wanted to marry. He will tell me about them on the fourth date when we are still in the auditioning phase, and I am no longer a paper-thin persona from the office, but a collage of memories and expressions and habits, someone he could care about. This is the period of sweetness and tenuousness. This is not love. It is antsy and easy and mostly performance. It comes with the process, just as you learn someone's scent and the feel of their hand in yours. Remember this: Love can have a steely or rusted or porous surface, or glint so bright you shouldn't look directly at it. Wait five minutes and love will change.

*

This is one of our best evenings together: a long walk around the park across from his house, which became our house when we married four years and two months ago. We stroll past the men who always stand on the shore of the pond, ostensibly fishing but content to never catch anything. The intention matters most. We hold hands and he walks on my left. He has known to be on my left since the second date. That is one of the reasons why I knew he was a keeper. We don't talk much, just a few words about spreadsheets—their endless tyranny, his eye strain due to the small print. I say maybe he needs a new prescription. He does not like the idea of stronger glasses. I shrug. A lens is a lens is a lens. He rests his arm around my shoulders to say maybe I am right. He has a light odor of sweat, but I don't mind people who smell like themselves. We keep walking. We will have thirteen more good years and two mediocre ones before the divorce, when he talks of retiring to upstate New York where he grew up and where his brother and sister still live with their families. Too cold, I say, even if he promises frequent visits to my siblings, but this is where my farsightedness is lacking. I can't see how to avoid the split, find a different trajectory, another curve in the path. Perhaps this is the blessed curse of knowing the future—knowing you can't change it, settling with the inevitable, continuing to walk with that knowledge in still-comfortable silence.

*

You can't tell a sixteen-year-old that their sporadic rushes of emotions aren't love but hormones. You can't work against the tidal rise and fall of their voices in the guidance counselor's office. Like the sea, that kind of surge isn't meant to be contained. I watch the daily storms while standing in the cafeteria line—the swells of pink affection, the steely gray crash of breakups, the soothing blue words of friends who try to comfort the bereaved, though it never works. Everyone wants to paddle out to the next wave. Like anyone who chooses to live by the sea, I am accustomed to the noise. Love isn't always crashing waves, there are calm places, lakes that are placid and not wind-whipped, where a boat could sail for hours undisturbed, but not everyone wants that sort of affection. More exciting, especially when you are young, to have the kind of lust that hits you in the face, leaves you near-drowning in the rush of being alive. Often, life is best realized when it is edged with death, or at least the illusion that one might be dying. While there are all kinds of lovescapes, my eye, unblinking, has no preference. It is not a matter of taste but change that must be embraced.

*

People change. Relationships change. They are like the ocean, never still, an idea that scares too many of us. Most want to believe in 'till death do us part,' that they can ride on the crest of waves and ignore the depth of the sea, a large and obvious detail. I never mention this tenuousness to lovers, though my reasoning is silly. I fear no one would love me if I couldn't say I'd love them forever, as if a love that won't last isn't worth having in the first place.

"I'll love you forever," my first husband said the day after we married, when we were both twenty-five and enjoyed trips to the beach, the idea of owning a Dalmatian, and had a great deal of contempt for anyone who played golf.

No, I wanted to say, *you'll love me for fourteen years, eight months, and six days, and then you won't stop loving me, but you'll love me in a way that means we shouldn't be married anymore, which is fine, which is the nature of love. It changes, it grows, it swells and condenses and divides.*

Instead, I said, "I love you too," and I did.

*

I'm not saying love isn't real. I'm saying it's alive.

At the End of Her Life, Eileen Watched *Keeping Up with the Kardashians*

This was the end before the language went, before she could no longer sit up in the chair. This was the time just before, when she could not eat but could still sit in her armchair and brush her own teeth. In the recliner, she put her feet up and watched Kim and Kourtney squabble. The women ate salads and wore sunglasses that obscured half their faces. When this was done, she would watch the bachelor handing out his rose. She watched the competitions, the dancing couples in costumes, the singers beneath spotlights.

Years before, when my friend R. was dying, I went to see him. I brought him the groceries his partner had asked for, ground lamb and spinach leaves and organic apple juice. He hoped the special diet would slow the effects of the disease. His bedroom door was open just slightly and I could see *The Complete Works of Shakespeare* open on his bed, facedown, holding a place. He shuffled to the dinner table with a cloth wound around his waist, unable to wear pants. At dinner we all smiled. His small daughter ate a plate of strawberries. I thought of Shakespeare and thought, *yes, this is what I will do. If I know my life is coming to an end, I will feed my body pure food. I will fight. I will drink the most beautiful words I've not yet read like water.*

Shakespeare, at the end of his life, retired, using Prospero to drown his book and ask for one final round of applause at the end of *The Tempest*, his last play. Shakespeare was forty-seven, healthy, famous. He wanted to spend time with his granddaughter. He wanted to drink with Ben Jonson. He had five years left to live.

Not long after Eileen died, I got sick, something the doctors could not diagnose, something the machines could not see when they irradiated my body to look inside. I believed I had what she had, some genetic TNT lighting its fuse from her to me. I looked at the bookshelves, the bedside table piled high. I looked at all the notes on my phone where I kept list after list: the movies I wanted to watch, the novels I wanted to read. I'd spent hours of my life, possibly hundreds of hours, reading reviews and writing down the names of albums and books and shows and films that tugged at my attention, waiting for time, for the gap in responsibilities and a precious string of hours to myself. And I didn't have the urge toward any of them. I was not dying, as it turned out, not yet, but I could see that if I were, I would turn my back on all of it. This feeling was not a fullness, like a person who has drunk all she needs and then pushes her cup away. It was a thirst so total that near the end, it disappears.

At the end of her life, Eileen watched Kim Kardashian crying about an earring she lost in the ocean. "Kim," her sister tells her, "there's people that are dying." *It's ok*, I wanted to say to Eileen, *to throw your best jewels to the waves*. But there was nothing I could tell her that she didn't already know.

Laura Mulqueen

Technique: The Empty Chair

Developed as a therapeutic technique by Fritz Perls, who (with wife, Laura, and Paul Goodman) developed Gestalt therapy in the 1940s & '50s

gestalt, n.: A 'shape', 'configuration', or 'structure' which as an object of perception forms a specific whole or unity incapable of expression simply in terms of its part (*OED*)

A reckoning: self:

Not the blue armchair   where
from him: you   retreated–

I left you

            –there

sit across from me:

            we   share
this striped rug this stripped
        memory–

            still
silent   carrying   you
I scream into pillows–
    for two   now

you made me   here

Gestalt psychology is an attempt to understand the laws behind the ability to acquire and maintain meaningful perceptions in an apparently chaotic world >>Wikipedia<<

Lift words   fractured in memory   quaking   brace

                                         in place   wait

          like water   absolved   in   waves
                    walk through   rise   fall

          under the moon   circular   passes

                    retract retrace {m(me)e}

My Favorite Felony: An Unexpurgated Account

The most poetic twenty-four hours of my life began with the first light of a summer midwestern morning in 1982, when birds sang my praises and dew jeweled the grass and flowed on like a river of mercury, each moment so right and inevitable, unified, a beautiful whole.

I had a couple days off from my job as a nurse's aide, and Greg, my twenty-eight-year-old roommate (who sometimes operated as a convenient boyfriend) was working at the Campbell's Soup factory. I had the two-bedroom apartment to myself, and I spent the morning writing away at my novel, which consisted of a file cabinet full of scrap paper. Enthused with my progress (I was just getting to the part where the main character, a woman with a beard, shaves), I took a coffee break on the front porch to relax and plan the next chapter.

My attention bounced from one thing to another. Cars streamed by; bright sunshine ricocheting from their chrome; dogs walked their owners in the park across the street; a distant lawn mower complained about its job. Three squirrels narrowly escaped being flattened. They dashed between the wheels and emerged triumphantly together in the park to laugh and celebrate, as though to show me that my own life was similarly charmed.

A string-haired man in a winter coat sat alone beneath a tree, gesticulating at the air and shaking his head. I recognized him from the Nebraska Psychiatric Institute, where I'd had a brief stay last fall. He went by the name "Red Graves Tumbleweed" until he was discharged. Then his name was Jim Davis. Apparently, he was now "Red" again.

I watched him repeatedly rake his fingers through his hair, as though it harbored small animals that he was trying to get rid of. I realized I hadn't washed my own hair in more than a week. I'd been too busy with the novel and working nights at Hillcrest Manor, writing ambitious lists of things to do, read, buy, eat, write, look at, talk about, think about, places to go, and positive attributes ("I have really good intentions," for example).

The last time I'd seen Red in the hospital, I was in a similar frame of mind. I paced the dayroom, my thoughts rocketing so dramatically no one else could keep up. I went nights without sleep; the beautiful energy of chaotic emotions finally yielded to powerful tranquilizers, rendering me ragdoll limp. In the interest of my own preferred style of sanity, I'd ditched those as soon as I got out.

But seeing Red was not a good omen.

Yet the squirrels were happy and safe, the dogs loll-tongued and eager, the birds chattering about their wonderful lives.

Just two doors down, the neon star at Madame Marko's Palm and Tarot Reading Shop flashed behind a greasy store window. I'd always meant to consult her at some point (maybe there was some actual purpose for my life that she could expose). Right now seemed a perfect time. I had a ten-dollar bill in my pocket and felt lucky.

As I went in, a bell jingled like a laughing baby. The dim room smelled of bacon and incense and was cluttered with candles, strange icons and a tall female mannequin in the corner, its stomach decoupaged with eyes and handless clocks.

Madame Marko, a stout, dark-skinned woman with mascaraed lashes like centipedes, appeared from behind a paisley tapestry. I told her I wanted my palm read, and she ushered me to a small, velvet-draped table, her arms jangling with bracelets and rings. I opened my fists for her. She glanced down for a second, then stared into my eyes.

"You have the Devil in you," she said, voice hushed with horror.

"You're not even looking at my palms!" I cried.

"I don't need to."

I was aware that my poor hygiene and the lack of sleep from slaving over my novel probably lent me some intensity. My eyes may have been dilated from the dark room. Even though I did not believe the Devil was responsible for anything beyond bad hair days, I found the accusation insulting.

Madame Marko offered a fool-proof solution: She could remove my demons by praying and lighting a three-foot-tall candle shaped like an elephant's tusk.

"Only two hundred dollars," she said.

The candle looked substantial enough to inflict severe bodily harm. How easy it would be to grab it and club Madame Marko over the head. "Blunt force trauma," the detectives would call it. And an officer on the scene would joke, "Wonder if her palms told her THAT was coming."

"What a bunch of crap," I said, undoubtedly reinforcing her diagnosis of me as "possessed." I leapt up from the table.

"Ten dollars for the reading," she snapped, palm open.

I stormed out, throwing the bill on the table.

The day turned sour for a while. I went back home and tried to take a nap, my thoughts pinging around like pin balls. I couldn't shut my eyes. They careened across the ceiling, where huge white hawks descended, talons out, to snatch my eyeballs. In the tree outside, birds no longer sang so sweetly. Now they scraped and rasped like knives on a whetstone.

I felt wrenched between the goodness and beauty of the morning and the howling darkness unleashed by Madame Marko. Perhaps I was possessed by the Devil. Should I ask her to burn that candle? It certainly looked impressive, and maybe her prayers had amplified power. Just because I doubted it would work didn't mean it wouldn't. I wondered if I could arrange a payment plan for that two hundred dollars.

I rummaged through all my drawers and pockets, hoping to find a stash of money I'd hidden and forgotten about, but I came up with only a dollar fifty-two in stray dimes and pennies. I confess I also searched Greg's dresser, yielding another seventy-five cents and a photo of an old girlfriend.

I decided to try eating, and I searched the kitchen for something that wasn't crunchy. The noise of my teeth grinding up potato chips or cereal might shatter my chafed nerves, but oatmeal and soup required dealing with the temperamental electric stove. I opened the fridge and drank the last swig of milk from the carton.

This led me to take the trash to the dumpster behind the house. One of my neighbors, an elderly man I called "Number Five" (he lived in apartment five across the alley), watered his scraggly rosebush with a bucket. He looked up and nodded at me as though he knew what I was up to—disposing of clothes smeared with my roommate's blood, hiding the murder weapon. Later he'd tell the police, "I saw her around two in the afternoon at the dumpster, so that must've been after she did it."

"Please don't turn me in," I said to him. His eyebrows rose a notch. I realized I'd incriminated myself. "Never mind," I added quickly, "We never had this conversation."

Back inside, I relaxed with relief. Of course, I hadn't murdered Greg. There were no bloody clothes. There was no murder weapon. Regardless of what Number Five suspected, I was innocent as a lamb. And I could prove it because I'd left no evidence in the dumpster.

The afternoon continued, sun blazing through the blinds in my bedroom. I sat on my mattress, cross legged. Thirteen slats of light lay across the blanket, and though I was not particularly superstitious, they stood out so prominently: lines on a page, an ancient text only I could decipher. Thirteen contained a one and a three. One stood for unity, three stood for the Trinity. My task in life was to bring all forces together in the interest of Good, and do it quietly, so no one would really notice until I finished. I realized that if I announced what I was doing, people would think I was crazy, and that would wreck my credibility.

My grand duty infused me with strength. I would go out of the house again. Bravely, I'd walk the plank over the fiery commotions of human agony, quelling the flames of misery that enveloped my fellow beings. Yes! The Universe hung between rebirth and annihilation. Yes! The time for action was now!

I surged down the street, blasts of hot wind raking my matted hair. I passed Madame Marko's, tempted to stop in and let her see the savior in my eyes. How would she react? Perhaps my powers burned too intensely for her. She might wither and curl like a dried-up rose. My first act of compassion was to let her be.

I'd left the apartment barefoot. I had no need for shoes. They were an impediment to my grasp of the earth, a requirement for saving the Universe. This was fine while I walked on the grass in the park, but when I crossed Farnam Street, the asphalt scorched and gravel and glass bit into my soles.

Physical pain could not deter me from the important mission ahead. I drove my feet into the pavement more forcefully, entertaining the notion that I could be "a martyr without a cause."

After a couple of miles on the sidewalk's hot coals, I sat down on a bus stop bench. Cars screamed by like silver missiles, bent on demolishing my good intentions. The traffic lights cycled through their usual colors, telling everyone when to go, but never where or how. Someone tossed a beer can from a rolled-down window, and it clattered in the gutter. I examined the blood and blisters on my feet. Now they just hurt, and I was tired and hungry and thirsty and didn't give a shit about saving some worthless world. The earth spun a little faster, like a piece of detritus circling a maelstrom.

Suddenly the No. 2 bus pulled up; the doors schlepped open. I jumped aboard, but when I couldn't produce the fare, the driver ordered me out.

"But my feet—" I said.

The driver snorted, "Use them." The doors schlepped closed again.

What happened to the rich beauty I tasted earlier? Maybe I chased it away with my overly ambitious expectations. I damaged it in my attempt to glorify my private fantasies of power and importance. Because of me, the Universe would rot and go to hell. I murdered Beauty even as I sought to save it, and I knew I could not assassinate Beauty with impunity. I deserved harsh punishment.

All right. I would turn myself in. The police station was only another mile downtown. I didn't care whether my crime was clear to others. It was entirely possible that the extent of the devastation might take a while to surface.

I entered the cool, air-conditioned lobby around six P.M. A uniformed man with a crew cut and close-set eyes stood up behind a counter.

"I'd like to report a crime," I said. "But I'm the guilty party. How does that work?"

His eyes narrowed. "What crime are you talking about?"

"I am confessing."

"To what?"

"I have assassinated Beauty and committed heinous crimes against the Universe."

"Oh?" His lips hinted at a sneer.

"I need to be executed."

"We can't do that."

"Why not?"

His hand strayed to the gun on his belt. He chewed his lips, cleared his throat. "Do you have a doctor here in town?"

This seemed like a ridiculous non sequitur, and I told him so. He suggested I "get help."

"This is an outrage!" I snapped. I dug my fists into my pockets to stifle my impulse to slug him. I imagined vaulting over the counter to grab him in a headlock, gripping his bristly hair in my crushing hands.

"You need to leave," he said.

I scoffed and turned abruptly away. As I stomped out the door, I shouted, "I guess you don't believe in crime prevention!"

I was all worked up now. If it took a crime to be punished for an even more serious crime, so be it. I kicked at a plate glass window, but it didn't break. I loitered for a while outside a drug store. I spit on the sidewalk. No one seemed to notice.

An hour or so later, I found myself in an alley, opening a door into a maze of hallways and small bedrooms. When I reached a large garage filled with fire engines and equipment, I understood I'd wandered into the bowels of the Omaha Fire Department. Men's voices and laughter descended from somewhere above. At first, I wanted to get caught. Surely it was a crime to infiltrate such an important agency. I climbed around on the fire engines, trying to figure out how to start one, leaving fingerprints everywhere. I pushed buttons to raise and lower the garage doors, tickled with my ability to control them. Several times uniformed men passed through, oblivious to the noise. Perhaps I really was invisible.

My ruined feet clamored for attention. Maybe I should ask some nice fireman to give me a ride home. They supposedly enjoyed rescuing people. But here was the fire chief's station wagon, keys dangling from the ignition. I raised the garage door one more time and started the car. No one noticed as I drove out, not even the police officer who pulled up beside me at a red light. I stared straight ahead and turned onto Dodge Street, rationalizing that I did not actually steal the car, I just happened to drive away in it. Besides, I'd return it the next night with my feet bandaged and shod.

The mercury streets rolled majestically on, and I followed them as I went, turning here, turning there, crossing the Missouri River to Council Bluffs, Iowa. Driving to Iowa City, where I'd been a college student three years before, struck me as a marvelous idea. But as I accelerated onto I-80, the gas gauge hovered near empty, and I had no money or identification. Temporarily disappointed, I exited at Neola and headed back to Council Bluffs, looking for a quiet place to contemplate my next move.

At dusk, I wound my way up to Fairmont Park to enjoy the lighted vista at the overlook. As I pulled up in my neon yellow station wagon with the OFD insignia on the door, two cars of nervous teenagers hastily left. Below me, Broadway stretched like a studded belt of stars. The jeweled skyline of Omaha winked across the river, drawing me to become a part of it all. But I needed to drive fast so I'd have more time before running out of gas.

As I descended from the park, I turned on the light bar and siren. I screamed along, cars pulling to the side left and right. I gripped the wheel so tightly that my hands cramped. I was a race car driver in first place, leaving all my opponents in the dust. I deftly played a video game, racking up the points with each car I passed. My jubilant laughter rose over the siren's shriek.

But the intensity didn't last long, and when I crossed the Missouri again, I shut off the siren and drove calmly to my apartment, parking in the backyard. I removed the keys. Greg was home by then, but he'd gone to bed early with a headache. I spent the night scribbling in my journal and adding a new chapter to my novel, almost forgetting the evening's events. Yeah, I'd committed a felony. Yeah, I'd go to jail, even though I intended to return the car tomorrow, and with my feet in such sorry shape, the police would understand. I began to hope I wouldn't be executed. Surely there were still good things I could accomplish. Even so, the crime was a beautiful, poetic whole already.

I'd slept only three hours of the last forty-eight, and my eyeballs felt gritty. At eight A.M. I heard a commotion in the backyard. Six police officers swarmed around my new car, taking pictures and dusting for fingerprints. They knocked on my door, and since Greg had already gone out, I reluctantly answered.

"Miss, do you know anything about this car in your backyard?"

"No, I don't," I said. I pulled the keys out of my pocket. "But I took these out so nobody would steal it. Again."

The officer gave me an odd look as I handed him the keys, and an hour later everyone had gone, taking the car with them.

It was a long morning. I wondered why I hadn't been arrested there on the spot. It was looking like I'd fooled them and gotten away with it. But I'd initially wanted to get caught and tried and sent to the electric chair. After all these crimes I'd committed, especially the assassination of Beauty, I remained at large, free to careen around breaking the law with more and more grievous infractions. I began to feel desperate. What did I have to do to be punished for my heinous crimes against the Universe? Murder Greg? Strangle Number Five? Steal Madame Marko's candle after beating her senseless with it?

Around two P.M. I got impatient and called the police station. "I have some information about that car that was stolen from the fire department," I said. "My friend took it. She'd like to confess."

The detective volunteered to come right over.

He was a harmless, mild-mannered fellow in a suit and tie, carrying a clipboard. I welcomed him in. After a brief conversation about my adventures, he suggested I go with him to the station. I eagerly hobbled out to his unmarked car, my swollen feet bulging my laceless tennis shoes.

That's where things get foggy. I recall a mirrored room, where I paced rapidly back and forth, impatient to get the trial going and move into a more permanent cell. My fingertips were pressed into ink and blotted on a series of squares. I grinned widely for the photo-ops. I even had an animated interview with the fire chief himself, who seemed clearly impressed by my crime. "No one has ever done this before!" he exclaimed.

Throughout the evening, I endured tight handcuffs and rough handling, more questions from authority figures, more arguments regarding my status. I eavesdropped every chance I could get. Evidently,

Number Five turned me in after all. He phoned in the location of the car this morning after the ten P.M. news advertised its disappearance. Greg had been questioned, and he knew absolutely nothing about any of it. The $10,000 worth of fire detection equipment in the back of the car had not even been touched. And I was to be admitted to the psych ward at the county hospital and placed in maximum security.

I spent the next several weeks there, drugged into apathetic submission by a variety of injected medications, eating shoe leather roast beef with a plastic spoon, sleeping with the cockroaches on a rubber mattress on the floor, peeing in a combination toilet/sink contraption, staring for hours at the crisscross pattern on my blanket.

The Board of Mental Health committed me to remain hospitalized until I improved, and the felony charges were dropped. When my mind began to clear, I felt deeply grateful that no one had chased or confronted me in the midst of my joyride. The consequences could have been even more grave. A few weeks later, I walked out of my cell, meek and complacent. I'd lost my job; Greg demanded I move out. I was discharged to my parents' care.

I'd expected to enjoy a high degree of notoriety, but only a very short news article appeared in the *Omaha World Herald*, mentioning I'd been charged with the crime. Evidently, the fire department was a little embarrassed that they'd flunked their security check when some crazy woman wandered in and drove off in their vehicle.

The true punishment for my crime, however, lasted years. The diagnosis of manic-depression (now bipolar disorder) supported the theory that I suffered from a host of complex symptoms that others found annoying, embarrassing, and sometimes frightening. Despite my fierce arguments to the contrary, authorities insisted that a debilitating mental illness had ravaged my reason and judgment.

The side effects of the medications they prescribed nearly suffocated me, causing extreme weight gain, sedation, drooling, urinary incontinence, blurred vision, and a profound apathy that I could not shake. My curiosity and ability to write vanished, every emotion dulled by this chemical lobotomy. I lost months at a time, sleeping and drooling, unable to work or go to school.

Often, my court-ordered outpatient commitment involved long-acting injections and close supervision by mental health professionals, who threatened incarceration if I did not comply with their wishes. This, perhaps, was the true crime.

But I don't want to give the impression that I always objected to treatment. At times my mood plummeted, and I desperately wanted help. The hospital offered me a safe place to ride out the storms of my symptoms.

Now, with the help of newer medications and my steady, supportive husband, I have come to enjoy freedom from psychosis, incarceration, and deadening side effects. I've worked closely with my doctors and caregivers, all of whom share a genuine interest in my recovery. As for the aforementioned felony, I believe I have served my time. I could have done three to five years in the Nebraska Corrections Center for Women. Some people might think I "got off easy," that my punishment was only "a slap on the wrist," but there are other more extreme forms of imprisonment. At times, five years behind bars seemed preferable to a lifetime of medications, hospitals, and being tortured by my own brain. Still, I cherish the memory of my wild and scenic ride, those twenty-four hours when life had such richness, such beautiful intensity. And as it turns out, the Universe has continued to bumble along just fine without my interference.

Kaleigh O'Keefe

Diagnoses and Misdiagnoses (alphabetical, incomplete)

adenomyosis. allergic reaction. anxiety. anorexia. astigmatism. bicornuate uterus. bitch. child. child of divorce. chronic. chronic pain. chronic urinary tract infections. common. costochondritis. crazy cunt. cyst. dehydration. depression. drama queen. drug user. drug seeker. dyke. dysmenorrhea. endometriosis. fag. fatigue. fibroadenoma. food poisoning. fungal infection. girl. good kid. growing pains. hysterical. incurable. influenza. interstitial cystitis. lazy. liar. liar. mononucleosis. muscle spasm. nausea. nerve pain. no cure. normal. norovirus. not enough exercise. not enough lube. not enough water. old for her age. onycholysis. overdose. pelvic floor dysfunction. poor kid. post-traumatic stress disorder. premenstrual dysphoric disorder. psychosomatic. septate uterus. shy. side effect. slut. smoker. stress. stress. stress. stress. stress. survivor. teenage girl. teenager. typical. unknown. unknown. unknown. unknown. urinary tract infection. victim. when you are older. when you have children. when you're dead. woman. woman. you'll grow out of it.

Latif Askia Ba

Bájalo

I sat on the floor of my walk-in shower.
My aide turned on the bath
but couldn't get the water
to come out of the showerhead.

Así, así?
She kept trying to turn the handle.

No, no. El oro, el oro.
I pointed to the golden ring
at the mouth of the bath faucet.
Bájalo.

Her hands kept going back up to the handle,
warm water coursing down brown tiles
as I laughed, the Latin phonemes
sweet on my tongue.

I hadn't spoken in four years,
the words left me like a pueblo
swallowed by seaweed and sand.

I tried to dig up dead words.
My shovel cut through
decaying limbs
smothered in ancient soil.

I held out my hand,
which shook in trochaic cantations.
Dame'l mano.
She gave me hers, and I guided it
by spasm
to the golden head of the faucet.

She pulled it down,
the water stopped,
her eyes widened,
then calmed.

The water poured from above,
and she thanked me...

I don't know why.

Your Very Own Low-Vision Dating Adventure

1

You met the girl online, on one of those dating sites that asks you a long series of questions about how you feel about messy rooms and vegan food and bondage and politics. You are, the website claims, 95 percent compatible with her.

This feels true when you begin to chat through the messaging service on the website. You've seen many of the same shows, read many of the same books. She asks good questions, responds thoughtfully to yours, has impeccable grammar. In her pictures, she's doing interesting things, like hiking up mountains, drinking beer against a backdrop that looks distinctly European, laughing into the sun. You try not to let your mind wrap around the word "perfect" when you think about her.

And then she asks you if you'd like to meet. Have dinner.

Your blood hums. This could be it, the moment you begin your love story, like in the movies you've been watching too often, sniffling when the music swells and the couple has the passionate kiss that seals their happy ending. You want this so badly it feels physical.

And yet, you're not like the couples in the movies. First, and most obviously, you're queer, and you're sometimes much more attracted to the quirky businesswoman than the disheveled fixer-upper guy. No big deal for this date, though—this girl is bisexual, has told you that she's dated other women before and is not just experimenting, won't stop you mid-makeout and say, "Um, actually, I'm not really into this. No offense, I think I'm straight."

It's the other thing you're worried about. You don't like the word "disabled," the way it feels heavy, makes you picture an overturned metal table pinning you to the ground. But it's what you are, what you have been since you were diagnosed with the untreatable genetic condition that is stealing your vision, bit by bit. Since it began to take hold seven years ago, there are so many things you can't do anymore. So many things you will have to explain to this girl before you can have that final kiss, which fades to black and opens back up with wedding flower petals falling around your faces, clinging to your hair as you bare your ecstatic teeth at each other.

You know that it's far too early to imagine marrying her. You're just thinking all of this because you're alone, and being alone makes you irrational, makes you skip all of the necessary steps.

You remind yourself that the last relationship you were in was also a result of terrible loneliness. That when the man proposed two months in and immediately after sex, him kneeling naked at your feet looking so vulnerable and ridiculous (you realized why people usually proposed with clothes on), you said yes anyway. Because you believed he really was the only one who would want to be with you. He made this feel true, too. Never said it, but made it clear in the ways he became frustrated with you and how you needed him to be your eyes. The way he sighed when you asked him to drive you to a doctor's appointment, to read the instructions on the frozen meal so you could microwave it, to help you set up the reading software that allowed you to complete your coursework for your master's program. The way he looked at you expectantly for a profuse thank you, sulked when you didn't express an adequate level of humiliated gratitude. And it was this feeling that you couldn't possibly do better that made you put up with the other things, with the nights he drank a whole bottle of vodka and then buried his face into the carpet and screamed until you needed to help him to the toilet so he could eject it all. With him accusing you of trying to attract everyone at the bar if you wore a skirt to meet your friends. With him refusing to speak to you for hours if you took a shower without inviting him to join you.

It took everything you had to escape him, to convince his mother to come collect him because he wouldn't leave your apartment, even though you said, *it's over*, so many times that the words just started to feel like noise. And you've been free for months now, which is good. So good. But the bed feels enormous, and you're ashamed of the way you miss his body folding around yours, the solid presence of him next to you on the couch as you watched your favorite science fiction shows, him reading you Neil Gaiman books at night until you fell asleep with your head tucked under his arm.

And now, there's this new girl. You're terrified to meet her, terrified that as soon as she sees you, all of the damage and loneliness and insecurity and weirdness of you will come pouring out. And it'll be over.

You decide to tell her you're not ready yet, that you want to get to know her first. Proceed to 16.

You decide to go for it, set up the date. Proceed to 2.

2

You message her back that you'd love to meet up. She suggests a place you've never heard of, but you ask if she'd mind going to a restaurant you know. You choose it because you can walk to it (you can't drive), because it has relatively bright lighting inside (dim lighting is nearly impossible for you to see in), because you know the menu (you can't read menus, the fine print impossible for your failing eyes to make out). You don't explain any of this to her, but she agrees to try your place.

On the evening of your date, you try on six different dresses before you settle on one that will definitely hide any armpit stains from nerves and working up a bit of a sweat in the half-mile walk to the restaurant.

You leave forty minutes early. This guarantees that you'll be there at least twenty minutes before the girl, so she has to find you, not the other way around. Although you've zoomed in on her pictures on your computer, you have trouble recognizing faces in person. Unless someone is nearly pressing their nose to yours, you can only make a vague guess at their identity.

When you arrive, though, the front door of the restaurant is locked. You pull at the handle again, then notice the sign. You take a picture of it with your phone so you can blow up the words and read them. "Closed For a Private Party."

Shit. You can't believe you didn't check ahead of time.

You can't contact the girl over the messaging service on your phone because, unlike on the computer, the app won't support text-to-speech or zooming in.

With your certain and safe plan gone, you feel a paralyzing swell of anxiety. You feel like your body is waiting for instructions from you to take each breath, to thrum out each heartbeat.

You decide to just walk home, and, from your laptop, send her an apology message. As soon as you make this decision, and turn away from the restaurant, your body begins to operate normally again. In your mind, you begin to compose, weighing how truthful to be. Proceed to 16.

You begin the breathing exercises you learned in therapy. Slow draw through the nose until your chest expands up and out, and dragon breath out the mouth. You feel calmer, and ready to give this a try. You wait for her to arrive. Proceed to 3.

3

You perch yourself on the wooden edge of the restaurant's landscaping, trying to look unconcerned and casual. You can feel little splinters snagging the ass of your dress, though, and a bit of yesterday's rain-damp seeping into your underwear, which is optimistically lacy.

The wait feels so long you think you might have slipped into one of those pocket universes where time passes at one-tenth speed. Your heart is doing an impressive array of nerve-related gymnastic feats which no breathing exercise can quite conquer, and you can feel sweat pooling in all of the most inconvenient crevices. You look down at your phone's lock screen, because there's not much else you can do with it. All of the text is too tiny and blowing it up and reading it word-by-word gives you a headache within minutes. If you had your headphones, you could listen to a podcast about the etymology of the word "muck" or the hidden design decisions behind mailboxes, but you didn't think to bring them.

Finally, you see a car pull up. Someone gets out, and, as the indistinct form grows nearer, you see it's girl-shaped with long hair. She pauses, then heads toward you. This must be the girl. She says your name, and you nod. She gets closer, smiles, and you're relatively certain that she is very pretty, just like the pictures.

"I'm sorry," you say, gesturing at the door. "It looks like we're going to have to find somewhere else to go."

"Oh," she says. "No problem. But have you been waiting long? You could have texted me."

You decide to lie. Proceed to 4.

You decide to tell her the truth. Proceed to 6.

4

"Oh, yeah, sorry," you say. "My phone died." As you say this, you reach into your purse, hold down the power button to your phone so it won't buzz later and give you away.

"That sucks!" she says. "Okay, I can look up an alternative. Gimme a sec." She pulls out her own phone, and you marvel at the deftness with which she navigates through it, fingers flying. "Okay, there's a sushi restaurant I've heard good things about that's a five-minute drive away. Why don't you follow me in your car, since you can't get directions? Where did you park?"

You decide to lie. Proceed to 5.

You decide to tell the truth. Proceed to 6.

5

"The weather was so nice, I decided to walk. I live really close by," you say.

"Oh, that's so cool!" she says. "Okay, I'll give you a ride."

You feel a solid twinge of guilt as you climb into her car, an almost audible click as you begin to accumulate your first untruths.

Proceed to 8.

6

"There's something I should tell you," you say.

She waits.

"There are some things I actually can't do. Like read anything that isn't really big, or drive. I mean, I could drive before. I learned how, on a stick too, but now I can't. Because of this condition I have that means I have terrible eyesight."

"Oh," she says. Her voice sounds falsely bright. "So, it's like being legally blind? Like, can you get glasses or something?"

This is a question you get asked all the time. When you're checking out at the grocery store and have to lean in really closely to see the prompts on the screen, the cashier will giggle and say something like, "Forgot your glasses, hon?"

You swallow your irritation, know it isn't the girl's fault for being curious, for not knowing. "No, unfortunately, there's not really anything I can do. It's a rare condition. I'm—" you pause for a moment, afraid of how she'll take the next thing you're going to say—"going blind."

"Oh." The word is stone-heavy, lands between the two of you. "God. I'm really sorry. I didn't mean to, you know—"

"It's okay," you say, quickly. "It's no big deal. I mean, it is, but I'm used to it."

She nods. There's a long silence, and you're afraid you've entered that alternate time bubble again.

"So, um," she says. "But is sushi okay? I could give you a ride over."

You decide to tell her you're not feeling well, which isn't untrue, that you're actually just going to walk home. She seems a bit surprised, but maybe also relieved. Proceed to 16.

You decide to accept the ride, hope things will become less awkward. Proceed to 7.

7

She holds the passenger door for you and shuts it behind you, all chivalrous. You wonder if she would have done this for you if you hadn't told her, if she's already beginning to treat you like you're broken.

"Is it cool if I play some music?" she asks.

You nod, and she turns on something instrumental, turns it so loud that it would be difficult to talk. You enjoy it, though, the way it folds velvety and thick around you. She turns away from the road occasionally, probably to check if you're into it, and you give her a thumbs-up and she gives you one back.

When you get to the restaurant, it's everything you'd been trying to avoid. Very dim lighting, the menus stacked with a hundred tiny options you'll never be able to decipher.

She sees you squinting at the menu, says "Is it hard for you to see? Do you need me to read it to you?"

You decide to let her help you with the menu. Proceed to 12.

You don't want to accept her help with the menu. Proceed to 13.

8

You pop yourself into the passenger seat, close the door softly behind you because your ex used to complain about the way you'd slam everything, never cautious enough. You notice with satisfaction, though, that she slams the crap out of her own door.

She holds out a cable to you and asks if you'd like to charge your phone and DJ. If you agreed, she'd see you put your nose up on the screen to find an artist, so you shake your head. "Play me something you like. Your car, your tunes."

"Okay, let's get weird," she says, and begins playing what she tells you is one of her favorite bands. You like it and tell her so. She tilts her face towards you, smiles, and you swear you can feel the warmth of it.

When you get to the restaurant, though, it's everything you'd been trying to avoid. Very dim lighting, the menus stacked with a hundred tiny options you'll never be able to decipher.

You decide to hide that you can't read the menu. Proceed to 9.

You decide to tell the truth. Proceed to 11.

9

The girl passes you the drinks list, and you pretend to examine it. When the waiter comes, you decide to order a gin and tonic. Every restaurant has a gin and tonic.

This one doesn't.

You ask the server which beers are on tap. He points to the paper in front of you, says, slightly impatiently, "All of our beers are listed here."

You feel color rush to your face. "Sorry. Um, any beer is fine."

"I can give you more time," he says.

Years of time wouldn't make your eyes miraculously able to make sense of the jumble in front of you. "Just bring me something you like, please," you say, and the server sniffs, leaves the table.

"I used to work as a server," the girl says. "I never knew what to do when people said something like that. I was always afraid I'd bring them something they hate. And it would be my fault.'

"I'll be happy with whatever he brings me," you say.

"Okay, good," she says, but there's a hint of apprehension in her voice.

The beer comes. You drink it. "Mm," you say. "I knew I could trust his taste."

She laughs, opens the sushi menu. "What are you thinking for dinner?"
You peer down at the lines of indistinguishable text.

You decide to continue to pretend you can read the menu. Proceed to 10.

You decide to tell the truth. Proceed to 11.

10

You feel heat flooding your face again. "I'm not sure yet. What are you thinking?"

She flips around, lists three dishes.

You grab onto this, access to the secrets of the menu. You repeat the dishes back to her, say, "Yeah! I was thinking the exact same thing!" You try to sound natural, pleasantly surprised that your mind would be so in accord with hers. What a fun coincidence to prove how alike you are.

She looks up, frowning slightly, and you remember you had just told her you hadn't decided. She's properly suspicious of you now, you realize, and she has every right to be. Click, click, goes your counter of untruths.

You remember what your mother used to say about lies, how each one was like a lead weight around your ankle. Too many, and you wouldn't be able to swim. You're feeling very heavy, the water rising past your chin, creeping towards your mouth.

You decide this just isn't the right moment to tell her; try to swallow the guilt and act as normally as possible. Proceed to 15.

You decide to tell the truth. Proceed to 11.

11

"Actually," you say, and stop. Your throat feels thick, your voice too high. "I probably should have told you. I can't read the menu."

She says nothing, but you can feel the bewilderment rolling off of her.

"I mean, I can read. I learned how to. I have a master's in English. It's just, I can't read now. Because—" you pause, because this is the tough part, and there's no good way to say it—"I'm going blind."

"Oh," she says. There's a depth to it, a swimming pool full of meaning. You want to go drown yourself in it.

"I'm sorry," she says. "That must be—I mean, it's got to be really hard."

"It's okay," you say. "I mean, it's not, but I'm fine, you know?"

There's a pause so wide, Evel Knievel would be hard-pressed to clear it.

Finally, she says, "So, about the menu. Do you—need help reading it?"

You decide to let her help you with the menu. Proceed to 12.

You don't want to accept her help with the menu. Proceed to 13.

12

You think maybe it will help break a bit of the tension if you say yes. You've read on a recent forum for low-vision people that allowing someone to do you a favor is a sign of strength, not weakness. This girl is not your ex, after all.

She begins on the appetizer page, going through each item slowly, looking up at you after each to see if you're interested. Her voice is kind, concerned. A bit like an elementary teacher reading to a student, checking for understanding. And you do feel like a child, shaking your head at everything, because nothing she's read so far sounds good, though you realize you should just pick something, or this will go on, and on, and on.

Soon, you're not even really hearing the words, and you just say, "Yes, sure, that one."

She repeats the item.

"Yes," you say. Then, "Thank you. Thank you so much. I really appreciate it. I know that was asking a lot. So, thank you."

"No problem," she says. "I actually really like reading aloud. It's kind of like performing. I always wanted to be in the plays in my high school, but I was too shy."

"Me too," you say.

"So you get it." She smiles. "But just reading, I can do. I was in this group in college that used to do community outreach kind of stuff, and we went to a nursing home and read like Charles Dickens, that kind of thing, and I'd get super into it, do different voices for the characters. And Dolly—she was one of the ladies there—used to tell me I had an NPR voice." She paused, did a funny sort of gasp. "Not that this is anything like that, of course."

But that's exactly what it is. You wonder if she's imagining a relationship with you as one long task that will earn her some sort of badge, like in Girl Scouts. Distinguished Helping of Disabled Girl. You imagine yourself in a rocking chair in your living room, covered in a crocheted blanket, teetering back and forth, and humming absently while the girl reads to you from a newspaper, and you saying, "Thank you, dearie. That's so nice."

You don't say any of this. "Dolly sounds like a trip," you say. "And you do have a nice voice."

"Thanks," she says, and nothing else, as if expecting you to steer the conversation from here. Steer it anywhere else, somewhere comfortable and safe for you both. You want to, you really do, but you can feel yourself transforming into Dolly under her eyes, feel yourself growing feeble, needy, distinctly unsexy. You have to say something very witty, very interesting and young and independent and cool.

Proceed to 14.

"I've got it," you say. You don't mean for it to sound snappy, but you're afraid it does.

You want to prove to her that you can do things on your own, that if you entered a relationship, it wouldn't just be you leaning on her all the time, depending on her to do things for you. You can still hear your ex-fiancé's long-suffering sighs, feel them heavy on the back of your neck.

You get out your phone, take pictures of each part of the menu, magnify, hold it close to your nose so you can make out each word. It takes a very long time, and you can feel her watching you, trying not to watch you. As soon as you find one thing you think you might not dislike, you close your screen, put the phone down. Your head is aching, like it always does when you try to focus on text for too long. You're also embarrassed, know there's nothing sexy about what you've just done.

"I hope you don't mind me saying," she says, "but that looks really difficult. Is that how you have to read everything? Sorry, I hope I'm not being rude."

"No, it's fine," you say. "I have a bunch of software I use on my computer, and usually I can use that to check over a menu before I go somewhere."

"Shit, that's not even something I'd think about. I'm sorry."

"You had no way of knowing." You rub the bridge of your nose, where it feels like there's an excavation going on inside your skull. You need to make her feel more comfortable, show her that you can have completely regular dates, guilt-free and fun. You can be so fun. You can say fun things. Now is the time to do it, but your brain feels sluggish with pain and shame.

Proceed to 14.

14

A silence extends between the two of you.

You know this silence, the silence of someone who doesn't know what's okay to say, and what isn't.

You know your silence, too, the silence of not knowing how much is too much to tell her about what it's really like to be you. How to be honest about yourself while also seeming attractive and datable, how to not seem like everything you're doing is just compensating for what you lack.

Or how to explain why you sprung this on her now, why you were too afraid to bring up your vision before, why it seems unfair that you would have to warn her in the chat before she'd even met you, that you don't want this to define her view of you without enough context about the rest of your identity, that there's no good way to tell someone, but a thousand bad ways.

Proceed to 15.

15

You make small talk, rehash the movies and books you both like, but there's no depth.

The drink you ordered disappears too quickly, before the girl is even a third of the way through hers. You wish for magical refills, for your mouth to do something normal. It's not doing normal things right now. It's suddenly talking and talking to fill the gaps in conversation. You're telling a story about your first dog, about how you made presentations for your parents to convince them to buy the dog, how you sat in the whelping box and picked her out on your tenth birthday, how when she pooped in the house, she covered it with a towel because she was ashamed. "And then, once, after a soccer game, we emptied the whole cooler of ice cubes in the yard. And she just lay there in the yard, eating and eating ice cubes, until she started shivering, but she just kept eating, until we had to pull her away." You force a laugh. The girl smiles politely. You tell three more dog stories. Then, you realize you haven't asked about the girl's dogs.

"I'm allergic," she says. "Though I'm kind of more of a cat person."

"Oh," you say. And then your mouth takes off again, and its cat stories now. Not even your cat stories, your friends' cat stories, and none of these are good or interesting either, but you don't seem to be able to stop yourself. *Shut up shut up shut up*, your brain says, but it's impossible. Also, too late.

When the server comes by and asks if you need anything, you say, "No." She says, "The check."

She insists on paying. She's got a very good job, one that allows her to be creative and problem-solve and lead teams in projects that create positive change, a job that makes the world better and makes her a lot of money. You don't object to her paying, though you feel you probably should. But reading the miniscule numbers on the receipt is also impossible without a production for you, so you watch as her card is whisked away, and then as she signs, businesslike and final.

When you get up from the booth, she hugs you in a way that feels pitying. You might be projecting, because you are feeling pretty self-pitying at the moment. She smells incredible, like cinnamon and roses and success, and her back is strong and tight. You know this is the only contact you'll ever have with her, and you force yourself not to hold on too long, sniff too deeply, be generally weird.

She says she can give you a ride home, but you can't stand accepting the empty kindness of this offer. Instead, you pretend you have to go to the bathroom so she'll leave ahead of you. Tucked into a stall that has a distinct whiff of recent feces, you get the phone close enough to your face to call an Uber home.

Proceed to 16.

Your apartment feels a particular kind of empty, the emptiness that comes from knowing you could be not alone, if things were different. If you were different—or, rather, undifferent in the right ways.

You usually don't let yourself be sorry for yourself, because it so clearly doesn't help you get through life as a functional human. However, you're feeling a deep sinkhole opening in your inner landscape. You sidle up to the jagged edge, look down. There's a definitive bottom, and you figure you can probably scramble back out of it by Monday, when you need to put on your professional face, which needs to be smooth and seamless.

Okay, you tell yourself. One night. Let's do this.

You pull out the prepackaged cookie dough you bought while imagining a second stay-in date with the girl, one where you'd bump into each other playfully while baking, bopping each other on the nose with oven mitts. You smash the image, push the pieces of it into the sinkhole ahead of you.

You settle into the couch and put on one of those happy-ending romantic movies with the happy, straight, non-disabled people, open the cookie dough, and chow down.

You shout angry things at the characters. Tell them how easy they have it, because they're not you. You let yourself cry in between noisily licking your fingers. Really cry, the kind that takes up your whole body, that makes your lungs knock against your ribs and curls your toes and leaves your jaw tired from allowing the sadness to escape through it. *Alone, alone, alone,* your mind chants. *Broken. Unlovable. Alone.*

You finish the movie and the cookie dough, and lie back on the couch, watch the ceiling like a blank theater screen, dredge up your own scenes you usually don't allow yourself to play. The day you were diagnosed, lights in your eyes sharp like blades, your mother crying. The day you crashed your car, peeled yourself away from the bright pink air bag, limped out of the vehicle that was crushed like a soda can, realized you would never have the independence of driving yourself again. The afternoon, two years into your undergrad degree, when you opened a book and it was too painful to make out more than a few sentences, your eyes refusing to resolve the letters into sense.

Sick from too much sugar and too much of everything, really, you fall asleep like this, on your back, mouth open to the dark.

*

The next morning, despite not setting an alarm, you manage to wake up by eight, and the sun is filtering yellow and possible through your living room windows. Your neck is stiff, and your mouth is sticky, but you slept hard like you haven't in months. You have the hollowed-out lightness of having expelled something ugly and heavy. Nothing is different, of course, but the sharpness of last night has diminished, become manageable. You stretch. Put feet to the floor.

You clean up the flecks of cookie dough from the coffee table, fluff the pillows, wash your face, talk yourself into eating the protein and fiber cereal for breakfast instead of the sugary one because it's good for you, do dishes, stuff your clothes from last night deep into the laundry basket so you don't have to look at them. You breathe, this part of yourself completely under your control, the steady pull and release, pull and release.

Proceed.

j.r. borja bridge, 2019

starry march night, a week shy from my birthday, an ideal setting for some romance novellas, except that it was the year i started trying to kill myself. in one of our sessions the morning after, i mention your name to my therapist. he says nothing and proceeds with a pep talk on personal boundaries and inessential baggage i should distance myself from.

there's not much here, that's what i conclude. but below us, the pitiless expanse of cagayan river in need of offering. we both agree that the color is mahogany red like blood extracted from autopsy. the river being the river is said to flow, to save us from sin, says an urban legend. thus, our age-old clamor to this watery grave: to wear the body, to desire the jump.

Jess Skyleson

Pyrophyte

I watch as the nurse lays out the vials,
tapping each, readying my IV.
Outside, snow has started to drift,
melting when it touches the warmth
of late-autumn city streets.

In my mind, these buildings rise
like towering sequoia:
their massive roots
form thick-veined arms,
gripping the earth
with broad, sinewy fists.

I flex my own as the needle enters,
feel its cold metal spark my blood,
resin-black, into lines of fire.
Once they have scorched my veins,
my heart becomes a seed.

Released, it floats gently down,
and I draw in a breath
sown deep with ash,
filling my body with the scent
of burning leaves.

Vanessa Garza

When My Broken Brain Misfires

My seven-year-old daughter Micki sits on a faux-leather high-back stool at the opposite end of the kitchen counter with a plate of heart-shaped strawberries and a paring knife in front of her. I want to reach for it. But a sudden gush in my stomach feels like I'm on a roller coaster moving higher, about to dive down and then around in an upside-down loop to hang for a bit. My body buzzes, déjà vu, an aura.

I grip the edges of the counter, waiting for the drop.

Hinged at the waist leaning over the cold white surface, the left side of my body turns warm. My left cheek, ear, and head burn red-hot. But I do not look different. No one sees what I feel inside, a misfire in my brain, a seizure. And not out of negligence. My internal signals are unrecognizable to others, like a lost hiker shining a flashlight in the sun. Indistinguishable from the light of day.

I look at Micki and my five-year-old son, John, sitting on the couch. The left side of my body, hot seconds ago, is now numb. This must be what a stroke feels like.

My ears hurt and pressure fills my head, an overblown balloon ready to pop unexpectedly, scaring the kids with its boom. Obscure sounds crescendo around me. The sound of our dog's footsteps builds like a fighter jet. The sound of John raising the volume on his show resembles a train echoing inside a tunnel. I hear Micki looking at the knife, soundless, screeching like fingernails on a chalkboard. When I say something in my mind, my voice echoes, simultaneously shrouded with loud static. *I'm okay; I have to be. This can't turn into something bad.*

"I'm having one," I say aloud. But maybe the words don't come out, or I say them too quietly, slurred. If I don't speak the words clearly, no one knows. My husband, Ryan, works at his computer in our home office down the hall. He can't hear me anyway.

With my eyes looking toward the knife, I smell and taste something toxic, metallic, like chemicals in a science lab. I have nothing in my mouth or nose, but I can't eliminate the scent or flavor. I can't spit or swallow or blow into a tissue to dismiss the odor and whatever lingers on my taste buds. This must be the smell of my sizzling brain. This foul toxin in my throat must be what the inside of my un-whole brain tastes like, my mangled brain held together with glue, plates, and screws.

I slump against the counter, nervous, although I know the heat on the left side of my body, the numbness, the noises, the smell, and taste are only in my mind as my brain fires a defunct electrical signal, a seizure in my temporal lobe. The lobe where a rare blood vessel malformation resided until 2017 when, at thirty-seven, my neurosurgeon drilled, sawed, scooped, scraped, and resected a potentially fatal lesion via four surgeries. Though the lesion is obliterated and can't kill me anymore, the scar tissue causes seizures.

I know I must hold the seizure in my barely-there temporal lobe, or I'll lose consciousness and convulse. But I don't control what happens next. I close my eyes, take deep breaths, and squeeze my fists—open, close, open, close—hoping my controllable physical actions cease the firestorm.

When a seizure stays localized in one lobe, it's called a focal aware seizure. I'm aware I'm having a seizure, I'm not convulsing, and I'm awake to talk myself through it, mostly. This type of irregular brain activity is also a warning, an aura, that a tonic-clonic (grand mal) seizure could ensue but is a seizure independently. During a tonic-clonic seizure, I'll collapse and convulse.

After a minute (my broken brain estimates), the heat, numbness, and hallucinations—sounds, smell, taste—abate, and I walk from the kitchen to the bathroom. My feet work. Even the left one that was scorching and feelingless seconds ago. My stomach hurts. Micki waits with her snack and knife, John watches TV, and Ryan works. Unaware.

Thankfully, I don't lose consciousness or shake in the bathroom as I did on the gray stone tile the night of my first tonic-clonic two years before. My eyeballs don't swivel in different directions and then roll back before my eyelids shut tight. I don't gurgle, turn purple in the face, foam at the mouth, or defecate on the floor, unresponsive, naked. My body stays calm. I don't stiffen or arch my back. I don't jerk back and forth against the porcelain toilet. Clank, clank, clank, as Ryan once described it.

This time, Ryan doesn't wrestle my jolting body or attempt to pry my mouth open so that I can breathe. He doesn't have to reposition my body to prevent me from knocking my head on the glass shower door. Bang, bang, bang, he once described to me.

My seizure that started in the kitchen does not evolve into a tonic-clonic.

I look at my face in the bathroom mirror this time, my right eyelid droopy, the electrical fire stopped. I open the Notes app on my phone to track this seizure with hundreds of others. I'll forget it happened if I don't write it down right away.

- *Monday, 3:30ish, standing in the kitchen. Felt foggy, got lost driving kids to school this morning. Went to bed late yesterday. Haven't eaten. Period starting next couple days.*

Thankfully, Ryan doesn't have to call the paramedics, afraid I'm dying. My kids don't have to see the red flashing lights from their bedroom window or hear the sirens howling or the heavy footsteps of the EMTs as they haul me down the stairs. Micki and John don't have to see their dad, frantic, trying to contact a neighbor so he can join me at the hospital.

"Should we book a flight right now?" my mom doesn't have to ask.

"Can we see her at the hospital yet, Dad?" my kids don't have to ask.

*

I know when I have a focal aware seizure, I'm likely to have more in the hours and days that follow. I worry because I can't trust my body or mind. I ask my daughter to tell me if I take a wrong turn on the drive to her dance class. I ask my son to check his math homework; I might miss something in my review. I tell Ryan that we'll order dinner, but he must call because I might forget what everyone wants.

I am frustrated when no one recognizes what happens to me when the focal seizures strike. Only I know. My family, naïve. I do not look different or sound alien. If I told you a seizure was happening and warned you, if the words made it out of my mouth, you wouldn't recognize anything abnormal. You might not believe me because you cannot see what I feel inside. Maybe it's better if I convulse so then you'll know.

I had six focal aware seizures the day our dog died, two the day after my birthday, and five sitting on the couch on a random day in January. I had dozens during the days before Christmas, wrapping presents with the door shut.

They happen in the car sometimes. They happen when I stay up too late. When I write, they happen, as I'm trying to get my words and feelings on the page. My doctor says I should sleep more. My family says I sleep too much. They tell me I don't need that much sleep, it's all in my head, I get enough sleep already. Yes, it is in my head, in my asymmetrical brain, where one side is smaller than the other, where a hole exists, where seizures remind me that I'm scarred, damaged, inadequate. My hearing, a section of my eyesight, bits of memory, my ability to comprehend, multitask, my emotions, and my confidence impacted. Some physiologically, some emotionally. I'm not sure which is worse.

Sometimes I practice life-saving tactics in case my focal seizures turn into tonic-clonics. How fast can I take the food out of the oven before losing consciousness? How fast can I remove a hot pan from the stove before convulsing? How quickly can I pull over before seizing with my kids in the car? Can I call for help and collapse by the door so the paramedics can find me?

The reality is that I won't know when a temporal lobe seizure will evolve into a tonic-clonic. They are unpredictable, and no one will notice until I'm convulsing and unconscious, foaming at the mouth, in a car accident, or burning down the house.

The focal seizures in my temporal lobe don't scare me. They are a nuisance. Like the one in the kitchen, they are quick. I know the routine—buzz, hot, numb, sound, taste, smell, bathroom. But the unpredictability of a tonic-clonic and understanding that only I recognize the warning makes me not okay. I'm a hazard without a warning label that's recognizable to others.

I walk from the bathroom to the office. Standing in the doorway, I catch Ryan's eyes when he looks up from his computer. "Hey, I had one."

"Damn it. I didn't know. Are you okay?"

"I think so. But watch me just in case. I need to help Micki now. She has a knife."

8 steps to survive a pandemic

1. Pull makeup over your eyelids and wash color onto your cheeks
    make sure if they stare
    it is because there is something to look at

2. because they will look anyways
    in the Tang dynasty, women would turn their wounds into beauty
    draw false scars across their faces
    no one can know the difference
    so no one can tell when you're hurt

    Like swallowing bitter melon
    Like the comfort of a plant growing around itself

3. Read an article titled:
    "Atlanta shootings reveal another side of Asian American story"
    and know you are too visible

4. Read an article titled
    "Disabled citizens left behind in US push to overcome the pandemic"
    and know they still will not see you

5. light incense to burn away what should not be there
    burn offerings to your ancestors
    and know they are listening
    know they understand because they too have tasted bitter melon

you can't help but wonder who carries the water
wonder who carries the moon
wonder if the moon is a bitter melon
and you collect the melon juice on your head
swallow the bitter and the cold

Wonder if they ate a melon if their teeth would fall out
wonder if they feel the weight of the water
or if we carry the moon alone

6. Drink melon moon juice

7. Drink melon moon juice and
   grow a garden in your stomach
   so you will have fruit to feed your laughter
   so you can grow a new moon to place beside the stars

8. Drink melon moon juice and
   grow a garden of melons
   cut them into slices to feed to your friends
   and we share this fruit
   at a picnic in mid-spring
   and imagine the overcast sky is filled with stars

Elizabeth Meade

What Happened to My Legs

When I was 13,
my legs slowly weakened,
folded like wings of paper cranes.
The knobs of my femurs started
slowly sliding from my hip sockets,
opened the door to pain.
My body screamed at the sharp descent
from the nest of independence.
I became a grounded bird
foraging for red berries, any bit of hope,
on the frozen ground of my grief.

By my 14th birthday,
I could no longer walk or stand.
Pain was my constant companion,
a chattering squirrel focused on feeding
from the same sustenance I'd found.
I came to appreciate his cunning ways,
discovered no matter how much he took,
he could not take my knowledge of flight.

When I was 16,
x-rays revealed dislocated hips.
Perhaps they felt as misplaced as I did,
just wanting to escape a body in turmoil.

I underwent surgery to pin them back home,
anchor them with steel.
In rehab, I relearned how to stand on my own,
to take steps with assistance.

Now, I am stepping into the light
on legs that are lightning rods for grace
and toes that know the soil speaks wisdom.
They curl themselves to listen.

Now, I fly.

Cristina Hartmann

What You Don't See

"Which would you rather be, deaf or blind?" Meredith whispered as we sat on our sleeping bags in her chilly basement. She had found the question in a chain letter, probably on bubble gum-scented stationery. It was what passed for profundity back then, as if our answers revealed some sort of existential truth. Maybe it did for me.

It was my first sleepover after moving to the neat 'burb outside of Pittsburgh where there were cul-de-sacs and pools you could only use three months a year. It was for my education, my mother said, so I would have more opportunities. Soon after my arrival, the popular girls rushed to befriend me, the city girl with a funny name and an unmarried Brazilian mother. Different, but not too different—that's the secret to popularity when you're eleven.

Divya, the resident drama queen, clutched her chest. "Neither! Both suck!"

I stiffened, and Jill's bold voice filled the basement. "A blind woman used to live with her mother down the street. Sometimes I'd hear her coming with her stick, and it was so loud. We prayed for her at dinner."

Divya said that she would be blind if she could play the piano like Stevie Wonder.

The girls' faces were lost to the shadows: that part of my blindness was already setting in. I raised my knees to my chin, wanting to hide like an injured cat, huddled away from predators who could smell weakness.

I could've told them what the doctor had said to my mother a few months before: "Your daughter has a retinal disorder that causes progressive vision loss." That wasn't how I thought of it, though. It was the things I tripped over, the whorls of lights that sometimes danced at the edges of my vision, and the flat black of the night. It was something familiar yet strange, ever-present and ever-changing.

Meredith made a low noise. "I want to see sunsets and my husband's face." She paused. "Do blind people get married?"

Her silhouette shifted, backlit by the large mirror behind her. "And you, Camila?"

My ashen and anxious face stared back at me in the mirror—easy pickings, the last thing I wanted to be. I turned away, flipped my hair like the older girls, and told my first lie of many: "I like looking at myself in the mirror too much."

The girls screamed with laughter and declared my answer the best one, filling me with grim pleasure. When we asked the Ouija board which boys liked us, I nudged the pointer toward four of the most popular boys' names when it was my turn.

*

My mother took me to an expensive *churrascaria* with tuxedo-wearing servers and heavy tablecloths for my *quinceañera*. We ate salad and barbecued meat with tender middles, and she told me of her entry into womanhood. "I had to wear an itchy white lace dress and heels that pinched my toes," she said in Portuguese, proof that she was feeling sentimental. "Your grandmother said that I should get used to pain now that I was a woman." She grimaced. "She was old-fashioned."

That was the year when my childhood chub formed womanly curves, and I started to bare my shoulders and legs. My mother had told me how all Brazilian women wore bikinis to the beach, from toddlers to wrinkled grandmothers. "God gave us our bodies," my mother said while sunbathing on our tiny patio, "so we shouldn't be ashamed." Things didn't work that way in America, where girls performed contortions to avoid exposing themselves in locker rooms.

That summer, my mother sent me to an educational camp to broaden my horizons and give me advantages in life. That was where I met Kevin in that haphazard way teenagers do, bumping into each other in the cafeteria. His normalcy fascinated me: his four-bedroom house in suburban Philadelphia with a trumpet-playing sister, an attorney father who smoked pot in the bathtub, and a mother who taught second grade. My modest exoticism proved equally enchanting with my incomplete family and my lightly tinted skin. What he liked the most was the sweet curve of my face. Cutie Pie, he called me.

One night he invited me behind the biology building. The darkness made me reach for him, which he mistook as a coquette move. It would become one of my tricks, touching men for stability and letting them think otherwise, but I had still been innocent back then.

It was my first kiss, dry and uncertain before becoming wet and sloppy. His braces scraped my lips, and I tasted mint. We fumbled toward a destination we didn't fully understand. My blood flowed faster, and I became aware of the smell of pine and summer surrounding us. His hot breath fell on my neck as he called me Cutie Pie, which felt like the ultimate compliment. After what seemed like forever, we came up for air with swollen lips.

We became an item. We linked hands everywhere, ate together, and rendezvoused each night at our secret spot. At night, I dreamed of grandmothers flaunting their bodies next to the nubile young women on the beach, gorgeous in their wrinkles and sunspots.

The summer's end approached, and we planned for when the miles stretched between us. We would message each other daily and traverse the state on Greyhound buses monthly. We would stay together as others unraveled. I began thinking of white satin, blue ribbons, and a happy-ever-after.

Two nights before our parting, he proposed a final seal for our relationship: "Let's tell each other a secret. A real one."

I closed my eyes and listened. Adam had been his best friend since nursery school. Adam told everyone that his family vacationed in the Bahamas when they visited his grandparents in Boca Raton—lies Kevin hated but never corrected. Adam also pirated hardcore porn and invited Kevin over to watch. "You know how strict my mom is..." Kevin said. They jerked off at separate corners of Adam's bed with the lights off until Adam reached over and did it for him. "I don't know how it happened," Kevin said, his voice small.

I thought of him, scared and vulnerable in the dark. "Oh, Kevin. It wasn't your fault."

"Does this make me gay?"

I squeezed him. "No. A gay guy wouldn't kiss me like you do."

His muscles relaxed, and he chuckled. "Your turn."

His confession made me brave, and I told him everything I never talked about. The words the doctors said each year: "Progressive losses in the peripheral visual fields." The unfathomable anger and guilt that filled me when my mother said *cuidado*. The way my mind sewed together the gaps in my sight and left me blind to my blindness. I spoke with my eyes closed like a sinner unburdening herself at confession.

"Wow, that's heavy," he said, and we sat in silence before he hastened me back, his grip tight and panicky. He didn't kiss me goodbye.

The next day, his hand stayed chaste at my elbow, and he didn't call me Cutie Pie. Looking around to make sure nobody overheard, he whispered questions during lunch instead of flirtations. Was I scared? Sometimes, but I didn't think about it most of the time. When would it happen? Nobody knew exactly, but by middle age. Would I be able to see his face? I... I didn't think so. Panic filled his voice, and I looked away.

We met at our spot one last time, and he blurted out, "You, um, live pretty far. So maybe we should, you know."

When his meaning sank in, my hand flew out into the shadows and thumped into his chest. "You... you pussy!" I hissed and stumbled away, sick to my stomach.

I saw him with his family the next day, surrounded by smiles and normalcy. He blushed when he spotted me, and I was glad that my sunglasses shielded my tear-swollen eyes.

*

Growing up, I watched my mother put on her face before work each morning. Dabs of foundation covered the discolorations from a childhood spent on a farm four hours northwest of São Paulo, where drivers still used hand signals. Blush to add maturity to a face she deemed too youthful. A shock of color—a bright scarf or a pair of dangling earrings—to remind everyone and herself where she came from. After slipping into her tailored suits and heels, she went from my mother, who was shy about her accent, to Dr. Ines Costa, an assistant professor of environmental sciences whose voice filled auditoriums.

Once I asked her why she bothered. "You're pretty already, *Mamãe*."

"Beauty isn't the point," she said, brandishing her mascara wand like a sword. "Men have their money and toys. We have this."

It was the summer before college when I understood what she had meant. I worked at an ice cream stand adjacent to a strip mall and a baseball diamond. After each game, the Little Leaguers lined up in their grass-stained uniforms for chocolate swirls. Their laughter mingled with the smell of freshly cut grass and spilled root beer.

My coworker Nick sulked in each afternoon, smirking at me. He removed his lip ring and covered his red-streaked black hair with a white cap, reserving his broad smile for gap-toothed children and their flirtatious older sisters. One day he proclaimed me Cautious Camila after watching me weave through the maze of milk crates and boxes of sugar.

My blindness had become something to outwit. I memorized the locations of stairwells and the number of steps, listened for approaching footfalls, and laughed away my occasional stumbles. Everyone smiled along, but my split-second hesitation always separated me from people like Nick, who moved through the world like they owned it.

As I waited for the bus each evening, he leaned on his beaten-down Toyota Camry with an arm around a girl, a different one each week. He watched me as I stood alone next to a spray-painted bus stop sign.

"Hey, Cautious!" he yelled one day, and his black-haired companion elbowed him. "How come you don't have a ride?"

"Too expensive," I said, which was true, but not the reason.

If I had been in a truth-telling mood, I would've told him how my hands had trembled as I sat in the driver's seat. The machine underneath me felt overpowering, dangerous. One wrong move, and there would be blood and crushed metal that couldn't be laughed away. I applied for a non-driver's identification instead of a learner's permit.

Nick snorted. "Says the girl with the brand-new threads and kicks."

I looked down at the clothes my mother and I had gotten on clearance and flipped him off.

The bus arrived, spewing warm smog. I greeted Marta, who worked nights at the twenty-four-hour pharmacy and sat across from a sullen-looking man. Nick's surprised face receded as the bus sped away.

I hated him then like I hated the cheerleaders who did their makeup at stoplights and the men who walked into poles while checking their Blackberries. They could be careless when I couldn't.

One rainy day, the bus barreled past, drenching me in dirty water. Nick pulled up next to me, nice and dry. "Wanna ride?" he asked.

I agreed only because the next bus wouldn't come for another hour and my socks were soaked through.

"So, why are you taking the bus? You should be interning for some hotshot," he asked. I had made the mistake of telling him where I was going to college. His questions ended as he pulled into the parking lot of an apartment building more for students than families. We were saving for college.

"I'm not who you think I am," I said as I got out, the dusk turning everything gray.

His rides became a ritual full of long detours along Pittsburgh's winding roads. With the wind in my hair and trees whipping by, I closed my eyes and pretended that I was in the driver's seat. My mother wouldn't have approved. "*Cuidado*, you can get carried away," she said during the birds-and-bees talk, "I did once." But I wanted to get carried away, far away from teachers who announced to the class that I had a vision impairment, from my vigilance, from my secrets.

Nick never made a move, and I pressed my lips against his one night near the outlook where the Pittsburgh skyline glittering against a sea of dark. His lip ring felt warm against my mouth as he reciprocated. "Cautious no more," he said afterward.

We began fooling around. He suffered from bouts of chivalry, asking me if I was sure every time we were about to cross a boundary.

The condom wrapper crinkled in my hand as I told him to get on with it. That is one of the things about going blind—it teaches you preparedness, thinking ahead, which came in handy.

Despite his faults, Nick was a considerate lover. He steadied me when I made a clumsy move and never rushed me. His touch was gentle, even if his words weren't. Afterward, we clung to each other in the cramped backseat, our bodies and scents tangled together, breathing hard. I marveled at the pleasure my body brought us both, a power far removed from medical charts and prognoses.

On my last day at work, I kissed Nick goodbye before heading to the bus stop. I could feel him watching as I walked away, and I wanted him to remember me like this forever—a mysterious and beautiful woman in the distance with the wind in her hair.

*

My mother only spoke of my father when she'd had too much wine, which was almost never. Two nights before my first day of college, I found her with a bottle of vinho verde. Her voice was soft, almost slurred: "Sometimes I wonder if I should've told your father about you, but it seemed impossible. He wanted to go back, and I wanted to stay." Her face was scrubbed clean of makeup, revealing burgeoning wrinkles around her eyes. Then she laughed, "This is just foolish talk, bebé. The past is past." I would soon understand that we are women of secrets, and we keep secrets for many reasons.

I loved my college years. There were no teachers to announce my business, no mother to worry about, nobody to know my secrets. There were only rolling hills dotted with neo-Gothic buildings amongst the oaks and maples, bright and inviting during the day, dark and alluring at night.

I learned how to welcome nightfall when everything was dipped in shadows. I followed girls' giggles to fraternity parties held at ramshackle mansions with flickering light fixtures. Pulsating music drowned out the hollow sounds of balls bouncing into cups full of beer. The houses stank of spilled beer and stale grease, the smell of carelessness. This wasn't the place where the future existed.

Sometimes I brought home a boy from these parties. Their touch told me everything I needed to know. The rough handlers cared more about their pleasure than mine, and the timid nudgers wouldn't know what to do. I chose them; they never chose me. When I made my decision, we went home and lost ourselves in each other. Once the sun rose, I bade them a farewell and ignored their texts.

It was all too easy to fool sighted people. All I had to do was let them assume things. The full cup of beer in my hand explained away any of my missteps. My roving eyes were a sign of inattentiveness, not of tunnel vision. They saw me reading regular print with glasses and asked no questions. Without the emblems of blindness, nobody could see it. My subterfuge felt like a victory until Eric.

We met at one of the shadowed parties during my junior year. He had a voice that cut through the music and a clean, uncomplicated smell. His smooth skin and gentle yet firm touch had me inviting him home. As I turned on the lights, I saw his smile. It wasn't lustful or possessive. It was just friendly.

One night became two, then three, and finally, we were spending most nights together. Eric liked to drum his fingers on my body, the where never seemed to matter as long as he was touching me. "I took piano as a kid," he said once. "Stank something terrible. But here I am, still working at it."

As he played a beat on my shoulder one night, he said, "You face things with such boldness," making me smile and think of myself as Courageous Camila. "The way that you look at me. Straight in the eye."

We stayed in this heavenly purgatory between a one-night stand and a relationship for three months until he ruined everything. He propped himself up on his elbows and spoke carefully. "Let's make things official. Boyfriend and girlfriend."

I pulled the sheet over myself, suddenly cold. "Why?"

His voice was low, almost hurt. "I thought we had a good thing going."

"We do," and I thought of his easy smiles and desires.

"Then what's the big deal?"

I didn't reply. He stood, becoming a hazy silhouette backlit by his lamp. Shadows encased his face, and whorls of light danced along the peripheries of my vision. "This doesn't make sense," he kept saying. I could feel his scrutiny, and I wanted to shy away. "You've been acting strange, always going straight for the drinks. You've been distracted, too. The other day you almost walked straight into someone at the bar."

"That was an accident!"

There was a long silence. "You have a drinking problem," he finally said. "Now it makes sense."

Shock filled me, and I tried to find his eyes in the shadows. "What? No!"

"You can't even look me in the eye."

My eyes hurt from the strain, and I let my gaze drop. "You know me better than that," I said, but of course, he didn't.

"Camila," he said, gently this time. "You can beat this." He spoke of programs and positive thinking exercises, his words fast and eager. The more he spoke, the tenser I became. "You'll get better. I promise."

His benediction echoed in my ears, and rage rose up in me. The shriek came before I could stop it. "Not everything gets better!"

"Wha—" he didn't get the rest out before I stumbled away, full of panic. Somehow, I got home, my shirt on backward and my throat tight.

I held the phone as it buzzed and tried to conjure explanations that never came. How could I justify omissions to someone so damn genuine? How could I tell him that some things cannot be fixed? That I didn't want his sincerity to fade? That I didn't know if he could handle the truth? He stopped calling, and I watched him pair off with a girl with a sunny smile and a steady gaze. It was for the best, I thought. He lived in a world where things were clear and simple; I lived in a murkier place.

*

When my mother was thirteen, she visited a cancer-stricken neighbor daily. What began as polite neighborliness became something more. The woman had four sons and no daughters. "I love my sons, but they cannot understand me in the way a daughter can." They played *buraco*, the woman dispensing life lessons as she laid down a suit of diamonds for the win.

One dusty afternoon, the neighbor pushed a shot glass of cachaça across the table and told my mother to drink up. "Women need to know their limits," she said. When my mother protested that it was unfair, that her brothers should know theirs too, the woman nodded, "*Sim*, but women suffer more for their excesses."

My mother went home tottering drunk, and my grandmother forbade all further visits, including the funeral. "My neighbor was a wiser woman than your grandmother," was my mother's conclusion. It was just a silly story until the second year of my doctorate.

That was when I began making mistakes. Helene, my dissertation director, a tiny woman swaddled in layers of nubby woolens, cradled my hand and said, "Camila, you are usually so precise. Is something wrong?"

The printed word had begun to slip away, letters mating to form new ones. Faces had lost their definition, giving everyone a blurry, unfocused visage. Instead of telling Helene any of this, I held her delicate hand in mine and promised I'd be more careful. It was something I had told my mother whenever I bumped into something or tripped. Outsmarting my blindness had always worked.

After an afternoon of words slipping away, I stepped into a bar for a reprieve from caution and thoughts of the future. My gin and tonic went to my head.

"Hey, beautiful," a voice said, and my coquette's smile clicked into place—a reflex. Before I could say anything, he sat down beside me and began blathering about Porsche Caymans. His inane chatter crowded out my thoughts of straight lines that looked broken, so I let him stay.

His name was Trevor, a master's student in the so-and-so department. His chatter floated past me as I thought of the way my mother's voice had brimmed with pride the last time we talked—"Camila, you are making something of yourself!"—and wondered what she would think of me now. When Trevor burst out laughing at a joke involving lasers, I joined in without hearing the punch line. The second gin and tonic had numbed my skin. I barely felt his hand on my thigh, my litmus test nonfunctional.

"Wanna watch a movie or something?" he said, something both of us knew was a lie.

It was full dark, and I had no energy to throw back my shoulders and walk as if I could see. I put my hand on Trevor's arm to steady myself, to reassure myself. He took that as an agreement.

As we stumbled toward his dumpy duplex, I tried to count the streets and turns, but everything blurred together. I clung to him for balance and guidance as he pulled me toward a place I didn't want to be.

Trevor was one of those men who thought making noises and rubbing a woman's skin raw were arousing. He kept telling me that I loved it as if he could telegraph it into my mind. Words like beautiful, hot, gorgeous came out of his mouth, and I felt none of the above. When he finished, I felt disgusted with him and myself.

I shivered in the strange bed and wished I was at home. I could list reasons why I didn't leave: the gin sloshing around in my stomach and mind, the late hour, and the fact that I didn't know my way home. All of that was true, but most of all, I was afraid of stumbling in the dark.

Around three A.M., he pinched my nipple, and pain sparked in my breast as my body awoke from its numbness. All I wanted was for daylight to come so I could escape. So, I turned away.

"C'mon," he said, and the word *no* got stuck in my throat.

I lay prone on the bed for a long time afterward, wondering when Cutie Pie Camila, Cautious Camila, and Courageous Camila had abandoned me. I reached out into the darkness, perhaps to find one of them. My hand thumped into a dresser. I stood on shaky legs and inched toward where I thought the door was, bumping against a floor lamp and a chair along the way. My hands roving along edges and surfaces, I finally reached my destination, the doorknob cool and reassuring in my hand. I wished for a white cane for the first time in my life to feel my way out.

His confused voice came: "What are you patting around like that for?" His laughter filled the small room.

I held myself still. The charade was over, and I spoke the words that had been locked up all along. "I'm blind, and I'm leaving!"

After a long pause and confirmations that I must be joking, Trevor babbled about not realizing that I had such a condition. His clumsy hands tried to guide me down the stairs, and I told him to drive me home, which he did without complaint. When I got out, he said, "I wouldn't have... If I had known."

I slammed the door and patted my way home. Surrounded by familiarity, I allowed the tears to flow until they ran dry.

It took me two days to tell Helene, who took my hand in hers and said to take the time I needed to get my affairs in order. "My dear, pretending takes so much work." She patted my hand. "Imagine what you could do when you stop."

*

My mother's voice rises in delight. "Oh, *bebé*! The purple one goes perfectly with your gray suit. This is the one."

I smile at my hazy reflection, the powdery smell of foundation still in my nose. Today is my dissertation defense, the day that I show what I have learned and done. My purple-tipped cane is poised in front of me, straight and elegant like a parasol. Kayla, my friend who is also blind and a minimalist, says I have too many canes, all in different colors. I tell her that we all need our vanities. With the final touch in place, I am ready.

My mother sighs, a sound of pride edged with sadness. I have told her everything, and she wishes that things were easier for me. It is a guilt I cannot absolve.

"I'll be all right," I tell her, and she squeezes my hand.

I walk toward the bus stop, my purple-tipped cane gliding over the cracks. The wind ruffles my hair as I come to the intersection, alert to the hum of traffic.

A wheezy voice emerges from behind: "Are you lost?"

A moment of doubt hits me, and I review my every step and turn. No, I hadn't made a mistake. I am exactly where I want to be, I reassure the middle-aged woman.

"Are you sure?" she asks.

There is nothing else to do except smile and thank her without meaning it. Cars roar forward, and it is my cue. I cross the street, my cane sweeping my way across. When the tip hits the curb, I step upward, steady and sure. But I know it doesn't matter. She can see only the white cane, not my suit or laptop bag full of knowledge.

I glimpse my reflection in a nearby window, a dark smudge against a sea of brightness, distorted and formless. Is this what everyone thinks of me? I close my eyes and think of the girl from that long-ago slumber party, brash and scared in equal measure. My body relaxes, and I allow myself to feel. The pulse of my heartbeat. The speed of my thoughts. The steadiness of my hand on the cane's rubber handle. I open my eyes to the hazy daylight and flip my hair like old times. With a smile, I extend my white cane and begin to walk.

Colleen Abel

At Central State Hospital, Virginia

Not fit for a lady to see.
But I saw, in Father's *Britannica*:
the ram's head, in one dimension,
black lines on sepia paper, in the center
of the woman's body.

My own body still in bloomers
and sailor suits. And, now I knew,
secret keeper of the ram's head,
horns snug fit to hips, bulbed
at their ends like bolls of cotton.

Later, when my mind went
sideways, the nurses brought
me chloroform in the white room.
As my sight bled, I heard them
murmur to each other: *unfit, unfit.*

Pastor had told us the devil
has goat's horns. Revelations said so.
When I learned what the doctors
had taken from me, I screamed
until my voice went black. Father

told me I should thank them, every
man who bladed that severing, every
woman who covered my mouth. Whose
bodies, then, are temples? Whose
driven flocks?

Chisom Okafor

a piercing through the dark

In the face of darkness, this secluded space is a pathology
likewise to live alone in it.
My heart keeps failing in bits, as the voice from the evening news,
crisp as snowflakes, announces that Twitter
has just been banned in my country.
It's close to bedtime, and my lover is on his knees,
hunched over the bed on the other side
praying in a language only he understands.

Empty tonight, I remember walking with my father to the cardiologist
six years ago, after I'd fallen for the fourth time,
off the cliff of a hill,
my feet devoid of sensations, my head swirling
as in a circumventing tornado.
When the doctor asked me to describe the pain in my chest,
I said: *angina.*
I said: *pectoris.*
I said: *there is an elephant on my chest.*
I can't remember which now.
But I'm sure he heard: *my heart is clean and white as silk.*
And muttered in reply: *I know. I know.*

After praying, my lover tells me he feels God has listened too much
to my arrhythmic heartbeats,
God sees your racing heart, he whispers.
Why not tell him something he has never seen?

He proceeds to talk to God instead, about Twitter,
and starts with: *a country, velvety red. Blood red.*
Red of the marooned. Red of the shipwrecked.
Red of oxygenated blood,
stuck within the perimeters of an endangered heart.

There is a trembling inside the both of us. A trembling precipitated
by silence.
We can't find more words for God than these.
This is where language ends. This is where language begins.

Sarah Allen

Hard of Hearing

I love you like a cat's ear
twitches—
with every angling
of myself toward
sound.
You are the percussion
that beats back
exponential silence
and, finally, leads it
to the firing squad.
My beloved tinnitus,
all your timbre and wave.
There is so much bang
and blood

My Father's Feet

The cinder block walls were painted "soothing blue," and the windows, heavy and industrial, were swathed in cheerful, frayed calico. Autumnal chill from the age-worn linoleum floor penetrated my socks as I paced. It was my night to wait and watch. I'd read a little, eaten so many pudding cups I'd lost count, and watched sitcoms to lighten my mood. I was exhausted but couldn't sleep. Sleeping on death watch felt like betrayal.

"I'm on Dad duty tonight; I'm fine," I told my mother and sister when I sent them home hours earlier. I'd been here before. Not in this room, but here, with death. I knew what to expect. And yet, I didn't know. Every death, like every birth, is different. I'd seen both, and I prided myself on maintaining detachment but also had cultivated a sense of awe at the responsibility of being present. I abhor flowery euphemisms about death. No passing away or rainbow bridges. We are born. We die. And if we're lucky, there are many good decades between the two.

I knew the nail polish remover odor bodies produce as they begin to die. I'd heard gurgling death rattles as patients' breathing became irregular. I understood the mottled patches of skin and cool extremities meant that the heart was no longer circulating blood effectively. I knew that patients supposedly don't sense thirst as death draws near, even if they haven't had a sip of water in a week. And because I knew, I thought I was safe from messy emotions. I'd worked part-time in hospice, so death watch cockiness came easily.

My dad was old school Catholic. He believed he was going to Heaven. People who got abortions and divorces weren't. When I was eight, I had a dog that was hit by a car and died. I was devastated but found comfort in God. For days, I prayed for my dog's soul to go to Heaven. I imagined God playing fetch with dogs. I couldn't wait to get there myself. A couple weeks later, I told my father I'd been praying, and Mingo's soul was in Heaven where he and his canine friends were hanging out with God.

"Animals don't have souls," my father responded. No emotion. Just a statement of fact according to Dad.

Even today, I wonder what possesses an adult to say that to a grieving child. Ignorance or die-hard belief? What kind of God destroys childhood wonder? I decided, at eight, that I was no longer Catholic if God didn't admit dogs to Heaven. Thus began my decades-long atheist chapter. Dad was steadfast, and I was wrong for daring to question God's will. I would be forced to attend church every Sunday, to be confirmed in the Catholic Church, and to keep my questions to myself.

"You just have to have faith," Dad said in response to hard spiritual questions. If asking complicated questions about God was bad, why, then, had God given me a brain? I had no faith in Dad's God.

A couple decades after my breakup with God, my daughter was born at home in my living room. My then-husband and I decided not to christen her because it felt meaningless. We felt it should be her decision when she was older. My dad was convinced I was damning her soul to eternity in purgatory or wherever unbaptized babies go.

"Well, baptism isn't just a Catholic thing. It's a Christian thing," my father told me, in that superior tone he often used when discussing God.

"I know. We believe she should decide *if* she wants to be Christian," I'd responded.

"Well, a layperson can baptize a child..." He seemed pleased with his not-so-veiled threat.

"If you baptize my child without my permission, you would be disrespectful, and I will never forgive you," I told him, furious.

Seven years later, he spontaneously announced, "We baptized her." He said it casually as if he were talking about the weather with that self-satisfied smirk I knew too well.

I have never felt as minimized as I did then. And in my family's tradition, I handled it in a nonverbal, passive-aggressive way. I silently vowed never to forgive him. We never spoke of it again.

Now I was sitting there, watching him die. My questions about God and unsolicited baptisms didn't seem important anymore.

My left eye twitched like a dog chasing a rabbit in his dreams. I peeled my socks off and threw them in the general direction of the small cot which the nursing home staff had brought in. I climbed onto the narrow hospital bed with my dad, squeezed my body close to his, balanced on my left hip, and rested my head on his shoulder. I watched his splotchy chest rising and falling, verrrrrrrrry slowly. I heard the gurgling in the back of his throat. It had become constant background noise in the last two days. I found the Frank Sinatra station on Pandora and cranked the volume. He'd always loved music. He'd always had a beautiful voice. Sinatra crooned the lyrics to "Fly Me to the Moon" and I sang along softly until my voice broke. I couldn't go on. My singing wasn't very good anyway. I snuggled closer.

From where I lay, I could see tall oak trees outside swaying in the breeze of the wee hours of that autumn morning. They'd shed most of their leaves. I made out the shapes of two deer, rummaging in the fallen leaves. I described them aloud to Dad. I didn't think I'd be able to stay awake much longer, with half of my body hanging off the bed and my eye twitching at warp speed. Did I really see the deer or was I hallucinating?

"I'm here, Dad; I'm not going anywhere. I am going to rest on the cot for a few minutes. I'll be right here. I love you," I whispered as I clambered onto my cot and fell asleep immediately.

I hadn't been sleeping twenty minutes when I awakened the way I used to when my infant daughter needed me. The gurgling had ceased. I had wondered how I'd feel at this moment. I rose from the cot and cursed as my feet hit the cold floor. I couldn't find my socks. Damn it, I couldn't go to my father's bedside and walk on this cold, germy floor without socks. I had to find my socks! Where the hell were my socks? Damn it, I had a dead father to tend to and where the hell were my socks? Why was I freaking out about socks anyway? What is the protocol when someone you love dies and you betrayed them by being asleep? I couldn't process anything until I'd found my socks. I couldn't look at him yet.

I found the socks where I'd thrown them earlier and pulled them on. I padded over to the window and gazed out. Still dark, but not the black dark of midnight; it was a lighter, grayer dark. Some believe the veil between Heaven and earth is thinnest just before dawn. And some believe this veil between the living and the dead is thinnest on October 31, Halloween. So, in the pre-dawn hours of November 1, I chuckled to myself as the woman who hated death euphemisms and mushy Sinatra songs lifted the heavy window to let my dad's soul fly out into that space between Heaven and earth.

I'd read somewhere that there might still be some brain activity right after a person dies, so I spoke to my dead dad. I don't know what I said. I felt I should cry but couldn't. I sat next to him and babbled about nothing. I did not call the nursing staff immediately. I marveled at how I had laid my head on his shoulder and watched his chest moving less than thirty minutes earlier. And now it was still. Never to move again. Eighty-four years of life, over, just like that. I needed some time alone with the realization. I realized that, at fifty-six, I would be lucky if I got another thirty years. Ouch.

Dad's mouth gaped, but thankfully his eyes were closed. I tried to close his mouth, but it seemed stuck. I stroked his head and kissed his cool, waxy forehead. Then, I called my mother and whispered, "He's gone." It was beginning to grow lighter outside, and the nursing home staff began their morning rounds. Life did indeed go on, but time was frozen for me. Time was a big gaping hole, like my father's open mouth. I didn't want to leave him so I stayed, glued to the chair until I could no longer ignore the activity around me.

It was all over. All those years of work, family, friends, travel, stories... over in literally one heartbeat. What if no one remains after that last heartbeat to tell our stories? Do they matter? Instead of tears or words, a twinge of the seed of guilt sprouted in my exhausted brain. I fell asleep. I betrayed him.

I wondered if he was in the Heaven he believed in. I wondered if he was reunited with Mingo and the dogs of his childhood. After all, years after my dog died, Pope Francis had said that animals do have souls. Therefore, it must be true. I was vindicated, by a Catholic pope, no less! I wondered if he'd forgiven me for hating his God or for being such a disappointment as a Catholic. And my daughter's clandestine baptism; could I forgive that? Maybe. I realized I was more like him than not. Stubborn. Steadfast. Opinionated. Egotistical. Generous. Compassionate.

The funeral home director came an hour later. My mother and sister could not bear to watch them remove Dad's body. I felt a sense of duty to stay. I didn't want to leave him alone. I didn't want them to put him in a bag. I couldn't bear the thought of them putting his body in an oven, reducing it to ash and bones. When I told the funeral home guy I wanted to stay and help, he looked surprised, "Are you sure?" Yep, I was sure as could be. I took my position at the foot of the bed and as he removed the covers from my father's body, I held Dad's cold feet in my warm hands. I'd never touched dead feet before. I'd read once that the nails and hair continue to grow for a short time after we die. His toenails had lost their pinkish hue. The skin was smooth, almost plastic.

Those feet had walked in war-torn Korea with the Air Force before I was born. I'd heard the stories a million times, about Korean children begging from the American soldiers. I knew the story of the Korean houseboy whose breath smelled of kimchee. Even when the posterior cortical atrophy took away most of my dad's ability to communicate in words, all we had to do was mention kimchee and he'd grimace and we'd laugh.

Those feet, at sixteen, had snuck out and caught a bus from Hartford, Connecticut to New York City to hear Charlie Parker play at Birdland. How passionate Dad must have been to have saved his paper route money to buy bus tickets and jazz. How giddy he must have been tapping his teenage feet in rhythm to live music from the legends he'd idolized.

Later in life, those feet had danced with me to the live sounds of Dizzy Gillespie improvising bebop on his trumpet in New Haven. In the early 1980s, I was an undergrad when I saw a poster announcing Dizzy's upcoming appearance at Toad's Place. I knew that just as he'd snuck out of the house at sixteen, he'd be happy to sneak out of the house in his forties, and that my mother, who did not share the music gene, would not be happy. But sneak out he did. And we drank beer and listened to music until the wee hours. My father brought his copy of *To Be or Not to Bop* and waited patiently in line for Dizzy to sign it. I shook Dizzy Gillespie's hand and thanked him for making my father happy.

Dad's feet walked on hot sand at the beach where I grew up, without flip flops or sandals. I was always fascinated by how he could walk on the scalding sand that made me scream and run for shade. He'd say, "It builds character." My siblings and I held contests to see who could walk on pavement so hot it had turned to mush for the longest time without flinching. I couldn't do it for long. I thought it was because I didn't have a strong character.

I remembered Dad's feet disco dancing in the mid-1970s. After *Saturday Night Fever* made disco popular, my parents took lessons, much to my horror as their image-conscious teenage daughter. They'd push the living room furniture to the perimeter of the room. And then, loading the vinyl soundtrack to the movie on the portable stereo, they'd practice their moves in front of a large bay window that faced street traffic. I was mortified with the embarrassment that only teenagers understand as I watched them swirling, my dad gracefully and dramatically twirling my mother. She wore a shiny bright aqua polyester dress with a full skirt that flared out each time she spun. I was convinced my friends were driving past and peeking in the bay window to mock my family.

For the last three years of life, those feet hadn't walked on the ground. They would never touch hot pavement or grass again. They would never tap to the beat of a favorite song. After the last stroke, Dad's caregivers had discontinued the walking physical therapy, a decision I was very much against. But what I thought didn't matter. And in those post-stroke years, it was the feet of me and my siblings that moved. One of us was always there. Every. Single. Day. On warm days, I would take him outside and do laps around the nursing home, my father in his wheelchair and me pushing him while talking about whatever flowers were in bloom. We'd sing songs. Anything. Christmas carols, oldies from the *Readers Digest* book of sheet music, childhood songs, you name it. Then, we'd go inside for a dinner of puréed fish and vegetables, which my father always treated as a gourmet experience. Occasionally, I brought thick milkshakes made with real ice cream, which for some ridiculous reason, were forbidden in favor of Ensure "milkshakes," which tasted of chemicals and plastic. It became my mission to sneak in his favorite foods. I promised myself there would be no fatal milkshake accidents and then I became bolder. I snuck in a pizza and chopped it up into tiny pieces and spoon fed it to him. I wanted to bring beer and some live jazz, but cranberry juice and my singing had to suffice.

Isn't it funny how, in the space of seconds, our minds can retrieve memories evoked by just one sight, sound, or smell? It's almost as if my father's feet were a pointer to the section of my brain where I stored certain memories, an anchor of sorts. Touching his feet was like hitting the play button on a ten-second video that flashed each scene in front of me for a millisecond. I took a mental picture of those feet and stored it in the DO NOT DELETE area of my brain's database.

I held tightly to those feet and those stories. We lifted my father's frail body onto a gurney and positioned him in a waiting unzipped bag. My father had nice feet. Though his body had deteriorated over recent years, and his mouth was stuck open as stiffness set in, his feet still looked like Dad. No gnarly, oddly shaped toes or toenails. No hairy ape feet. I admired them one last time. I looked down at my own feet covered in heavy socks as the funeral director zipped up the bag and began to maneuver the gurney toward the door. I forced my own feet to move forward and followed.

And then I began to cry.

Latif Askia Ba

The Dentist's Caliphate

I went to the tooth clinic.
The curves of my back fought against the angles of the chair.
They took a while to take my blood pressure.
Spasms came as the cuff inflated
and ceased when the people stopped touching me.
They tried again and again,
my bicep beating,
the green veins inflating in my forearm.
When they pried my mouth open,
the professor explained how there was nothing to fear—
he was just examining my teeth,
my head shaking,
my feet kicking,
my hands grasping at each other
in a great effort to relax.
I said I understand,
and he said good,
his pinky on my chin,
his silver mirror in my mouth.
He kept calling me Kalif
as his dental students watched this rare case.
Sometimes I'd try to trick myself:
"It doesn't matter. You can move all you want."
But I'm not stupid enough for that.
My razor-sharp ego
Grabs me by the neck.

Becca Carson

Prayer For Forgiveness

If you are my judge
whose hands tremble
from the injury of this love.
Is it true we have created each other?
Look for me weeping light
in that wild valley far from Eden.
When I was nothing, I curled around
the galactic clay of your fist, fetal position
with no borrowed rib.
Lord, where am I?
I know only darkness, light, mourning.
I hide your wounds
in my body afflicted
and though I doubt I believe
in forgiveness of sins,
I hope forgiveness, like resurrection of the body,
might hover in the air of our death, might sound
more holy than redemption.

Kara Dorris

Pin-Up Girl

This is my hot minute as a pin-up, golden
hour, center stage as my doctor presents my body scans

at his conference panel. My MRI
says *degeneration, need a bone scan*. What else can

a magnetic field, that momentary halo, show
as my body bounces radio pulses back. I wonder

why no one tells us the body is always ready
to receive frequencies since those song waves knock

us from our tables & upright positions constantly.
We should have known, nuclei—like us—to Marco

our Polo as they realign. That you would need a computer
to interpret the 3D of my reactions into less painful

2D images; my bone scan shouts in different directions
to see what echoes. Radioactive tracers congregate

in areas working the hardest to repair. Dark spots,
like mildew, surround my bright spine,

heat from implication not the sun, but I guess
both are just ways to say consequence,

like an avalanche gaining,
a shelf-life halving.

Hairline Movement

Against my shy nature, my feet shuffle hesitantly into the next salon; I glance around, hopeful for a staircase or even a curtain but spot neither. *"Excuse me, is Xie Shīfù here?"*

Two barbers look up from absentmindedly scrolling through their phones, a third doesn't move his eyes from the TV featuring a Han dynasty-inspired fantasy. The same response rises: Who? I repeat myself, stating that he's a masseuse. They shake their heads and one of the barbers cutting hair nearest to me pauses, scissors in midair as a lock of hair juts out, attached to the customer for the final second. *"No, but we offer a head massage alongside a haircut."*

I decline, apologize for disturbing them, and stumble out of this salon, the third I've entered on this road. How many more will I step into asking for this elusive Xie Shīfù?

After living in China for seven months and having just completed a semester in Beijing, I have returned to the first city I studied in: Xi'an. I visit for a week in December to see friends, frequent favorite restaurants, roam historic monuments I've yet been able to visit, and sip copious amounts of tea at the beloved Cháng'ān International Tea Mall.

I had asked a tea friend for a recommendation of a good masseuse. His instructions had been sincere but alarmingly vague: turn right on South Cháng'ān Road and he'll be on the second floor of a barbershop. My friend neither had Xie Shīfù's contact number, nor remembered which salon he was located in. When I asked for the description of the salon, he smiled in embarrassment. He had never been a customer of Xie Shīfù but had heard from a trusted friend that the masseuse was unparalleled. He suggested I simply wander down the street and ask until I found Xie Shīfù, as he couldn't be more than a five-minute walk away.

The first few salons I had entered were certain that I must be speaking Mandarin incorrectly and assumed I wanted to cut my hair and finish with a head massage. Exasperated, I exit again, unsure whether this is normal back in the States, as I cut my own curly, auburn hair.

I wander beyond a bāozi shop with baskets the circumference of my arms outstretched, which release steam as pedestrians claim their orders. After passing two banks and numerous clothing stores, I glance at the absence where street vendors once squatted over the summer. Within a few seconds, a dozen buses speed by; they are white and blue, some with advertisements, but all with digital, red neon signs indicating their route number. Lime green taxis and various vehicles with the Shǎn license plates honk in competition with the buses' basses.

I step into the next shop, pushing aside the thick, heavy winter plastic flaps to prevent cold temperatures from encroaching indoors. *"Excuse me, is Xie Shīfù here?"*

One barber looks up; he sports a rockstar glam with spiked hair. *"Which Xie?"*

"The Xie as in the character of 'thank you.'"

"He's upstairs," he points to a side door with dangling maroon beads. I nod, usher a thank you, then tiptoe upstairs.

When I reach the top, I nearly turn to leave. There are several large cardboard boxes—some are taped shut while others gape modestly, revealing various salon supplies. None are marked as fragile. Just to the side of this fortress of boxes are two massage tables. Charts of the body pinpointing meridians of qì and scrolls depicting the Laughing Buddha line the walls. A small window peers into the ten-lane street below. Two chairs sit facing the massage tables, cuddled into a round, wooden table sporting a large, transparent vessel brimming with a beverage of mulberry hue. The more time I have spent in China, the more I realize that the best places are truly obscure and nearly impossible to find. Master Xie's massage parlor is one such place.

I step forward, the gentle winter sun peeking through the window, dust particles lazily dancing in the air, and then a man in a traditional white gongfu suit steps forward. *"You must have been sent by our tea friend. Yes?"*

I confirm and he gestures for me to sit. Both seats face outward from the wall at an angle, which requires us to turn our heads in order to face each other. *"I've heard you're from Sichuan, is that correct?"*

"Yes," and he mentions a village I am not familiar with. *"It's about two hours outside Chengdu."*

"I'll be moving to Chengdu next week. I am very happy to meet you."

"Then this is our 缘分.[1] *I have just relocated to Xi'an this month so you must forgive this humble abode,"* he nods to the room. *"I am still setting up my business here."*

"Then this truly is our yuánfèn."

I open my mouth to ask about pricing but before I can, Master Xie asks: *"Where in your body is the pain?"*

I roll through the memorized vocabulary in my second tongue, *"The most intense pain is in my jaw, neck, upper shoulders, and lower back. The worst is in my jaw and lower back."*

"Is the pain standard or is it sour?"

I pause. I had originally mistaken the word for ache as sour, as the pīnyīn is the same. During my first traditional Chinese massage in Xi'an, I learned that 'sour' indicates aching pain that radiates outward.[2] *"It's sour in all these places."*

---

[1] Yuánfèn. Fate, Destiny, Serendipity. Yuánfèn is a word which entails the serendipitous meeting of two individuals. While the word has roots in Buddhist ideology, it is widely shared among 茶友 (chá yǒu - tea friends) and others who believe in the auspicious crossing of two paths.

[2] The words for "ache" and "sour" in Mandarin are homonyms: 痠 ache suān / 酸 sour suān.

"*Can you tolerate pain?*" His eyes are warm, albeit concerned. I wonder if he'll say what I've heard many times from doctors in the US: you're too young to feel this much pain.

"*I can.*"

He nods once. "*The massage will hurt, but in the following days, you will experience great relief.*" I nod, not fearing the proposed pain as I typically ask masseuses to apply heavier pressure two or three times during a session. "*Alright. You can lay down but first remove your coat.*"

I stand awkwardly. "*Shīfù, there's one more concern. I just ask that you don't massage or touch my feet. Is that possible?*" He confirms then shuffles away before I can inquire about the price. I timidly begin to peel off the copious layers of clothes: the winter coat, the inner jacket, a long-sleeved garment, until I have stripped down into thermal tights and a tank top. I snuggle quickly into the thin, white cover of the massage table and exhale deeply.

I notice my shoulders are pitched high and exhale again, coaxing them down. What's more difficult to ease is the anxiety over how much this massage will cost. Massage is a luxury. As a full-time student paying my own tuition while working four jobs, I have not been able to afford massage. But now that the opportunity arises in China while I benefit from government scholarships, I seize it, desperate for relief. I exhale away my discomfort, as it's an appointment booked via guānxì and I am a student, so I have faith that I will not be overcharged. From the rates I've seen in Xi'an and Beijing, hourly rates deviate from fifty to two hundred RMB.

Xie Shīfù returns, relocates a heating lamp over my body, and begins by making sweeping gestures lightly, then in increasing pressure. He starts at my neck, brushes down the spine, then repeats down the arms. Soon, I grunt from the pressure he inflicts onto my muscles. The knots lodged in my lower back are as large as my fists, symmetrical and demanding. When at last he reaches them, the force he uses to pull the two knots away from my curved spine is enough that I know I will walk away bruised. That is another mysterious, undiagnosed condition of mine: why my skin bruises so easily, often transforming a flick into a malnourished, violet blossom.

My breathing labors with the control to not groan. As he promised, it is painful; my teeth alternate slicing into my gum and lower lip as he massages my lower back. I am too proud to ask the master to lighten his pressure. My hip bones dive into the flesh of the massage table beneath me. I count my breath on the rotation of eight to ensure I don't pass out, elongations of 呼吸[3], a mantra for each hū and every xī. Then, Master Xie introduces life into pinpoints of my body that I was unaware of. His nimble fingers flicker along the flesh of my spine in succinct, staccato pinches. They tug muscle or sinew, or perhaps something else away from the bone. My spine cracks like a fire spreading over gasoline, whipping along meridians of my legs and through my torso. I arch my back, sucking in oxygen as if that can extinguish the sensation.

"得气了吗?"[4]

I've never felt this before. It's as if every meridian along my spine is experiencing qì for the first time. In epiphany, I finally understand what 'obtaining qi' means. It feels like healing fire is coursing through my channels.

"Dé qìle," I grunt as my petite body is easily rocked forth and back due to his exertion.

"那就好. 放松吧."[5]

The first time I heard fàngsōng was in a traditional Chinese medicine hospital in Xi'an over the summer. I went with a classmate who was also in the intermediate Chinese course. We both operated at shifting levels of proficiency: while we could write 500-800-character essays,

---

[3]　Hūxī. *Breathe*

[4]　Dé qìle ma? *Have you obtained qì?*

[5]　Nà jiù hǎo. Fàngsōng ba. *That's good. Relax.*

answering complex questions without referring to a dictionary was difficult. The most humbling aspect was learning, through immersion and circumlocution, simple words such as shampoo, chivalry, and preface.[6] Having since ascended into a professional proficiency in Mandarin, I now grin at the memory of how I first learned fàngsōng.

I had perched timidly on a massage table without a curtain in a room with six massage tables that served a dual purpose for those receiving guasha or acupuncture. My classmate found out the difference between 趴着[7] and 躺着[8] by flipping to and fro until an exasperated doctor laughed, *"Don't move!"*

When the doctor's eyes turned on me, I followed my classmate to pā zhe. I closed my eyes and exhaled a sustained breath to release the tension from hunching over a desk for the majority of each day of the week. She inquired where it hurt from my classmate, and he described the soreness in the shoulders and mid-back. To another doctor, I rattled off my recipe of bodily aches. When she began massaging me, my shoulders pitched up to my ears, my breath sharpened.

"Fàngsōng, fàngsōng ba."

Fàng means release. But what is sōng? To deliver. To deliver release? I wondered what the characters were and made a mental note to ask the doctor afterwards so I could jot them down in my notebook.

"It means relax," my classmate said, voice muffled. I thanked him.

After the massage, my pain reduced significantly. The constant throb still ached and refused to dissipate, but that was close enough to not being in pain, at least for the first hour immediately following the massage.

As we gathered our bags to leave, my classmate raised a bushy eyebrow at me. *"Should we tip?"*

---

[6] 洗发精 xǐ fǎ jīng, 狭义 xiáyì, and 前言 qiányán, respectively
[7] Pā zhe. To lie facing downwards
[8] Tǎng zhe. To lie facing upwards

"There shouldn't be a need," I responded. *"Tipping isn't necessary in restaurants so why would it be here?"*

"Oh, I see. I wasn't sure."

"No worries." I paused, swinging my backpack over my shoulder, and looked at the curtain shielding a patient in the corner. *"Is tipping normal in the US?"*

"For massage? Yes, of course!"

"Oh," I exhaled as guilt plunged through me.

The first time I received a massage was as a celebratory gift to myself for making it to twenty, alive. Aches and pains had driven me to indulge in a costly, but worthwhile, procedure. I booked a deep tissue massage and nimbly shimmied into the rich covers of a massage bed in a small room attached to the side of a vegan cafe in downtown Kenosha, Wisconsin.

The blankets felt luxurious under my nearly naked skin; I only wore panties, and being practically nude in public, even behind the four walls of this private room, was novel to me. Ocean music with crashing waves and sparkling wind chimes sounded from a small speaker on the bottom rung of a table. When the masseuse entered, I asked her to play any other music. She selected a rainforest-inspired track and the first of my tensions eroded.

After confirming where the majority of my high intensity pain resided, I requested twice for her not to massage or even touch my feet. Gently, as I laid face down, she unrolled the sheet until it was tucked into the crest of my panties. The sound of a lotion dispenser squirted. First, she coated my back, neck, then arms in long strokes to evenly spread the lotion. The smell of lavender essential oil filled the room.

I had deliberated between booking a female or male masseuse. Could I trust a man alone in a room with my body? No, I finally decided; I couldn't trust people I dated not to manipulate and invade me. Why would I trust a stranger?

I was surprised at the strength of the masseuse's hands and wondered at the depths of my internalized sexism. My muscles felt as if they were being gently tenderized; I forcibly inhaled to stifle the squeaks and moans that threatened to tumble from my mouth. When she suggested using less pressure, I declined. Whatever discomfort resided at that time would let me reap its benefits afterwards. When she pressed into a swollen knot in my neck, a sharp pain resonated over my right eye and a white light flashed behind my closed eyes. I gasped. "That spot tugs all the way into my jaw."

"Is it a stiff pain or a radiating pain?"

"It's radiating." She pressed around the knot in a circular manner. "I think I have something like TMJ."

A silence elongated as she pressed with increasing intensity into the knot. The pain seared and I bit my lip. "A lot of people mistake TMJ for TMJD. TMJ is just the temporomandibular joint," she brushed a finger lightly against my right jaw, the one with the greatest pain. "But the pain you're having is likely the disorder or dysfunction of the TMJ."

I nodded, grateful for this information. She continued in a melodic, soothing voice: "A lot of abused women have TMJD. They can't speak out against what's happening to them without fear of retaliation, so they clench their teeth which inevitably pulls on the muscles in the jaw." Her hands traced the muscles in my neck down to my shoulders, using medical terms I was unfamiliar with, and demonstrated how pressure applied in one part of the body affects everything leading outward. "Abused women often lack confidence and look down at the floor instead of up, so the muscles in the neck are constantly being strained. And that results, partially, in sloping shoulders, a hunched back, uneven hips, stressed knees, and weak ankles."

I laid in silence, absorbing the intersection of my selfhood. How did she know? How could she know from a single statement about my jaw that I had been abused?

I wouldn't realize until two years after this massage how severe my TMJD was; the pain in my jaw still meanders between excruciating and numbing. After getting x-rays to have my wisdom teeth removed, I was turned away by three dentists who refused to do the risky procedure. My limited jaw mobility was complicated by the roots of two wisdom teeth that had grown so close to the nerve, extraction risked potential paralyzation. The x-ray contained evidence that my jaw had long shifted into the final, irreversible stage of TMJD: the joint had dislocated, and bone was grinding directly against bone: the sound of sandpaper. The intensity immediately clarified why my jaw was in excruciating pain in winter and why I couldn't eat during the worst of the pain; why I couldn't chew gum, taffy, or any other sticky or hard textures; why I always took nibbles out of food and couldn't open my mouth wide; why I often had migraines; why I couldn't bite into ice cream.

"You're letting your disability stop you." An ex-boyfriend told me once, guiltily breaking my will to open my mouth despite the click and the shift and the surge in pain to perform fellatio. I couldn't take much in and my gag reflex forced me to bite down on him. He yelped like a puppy. I apologized, but a cruel part of me was thankful for my reflex, as if it was a self-defense mechanism.

While he never again asked for head, I was left wondering: Do I allow my body to stop me from doing what I want? What, then, about what I don't want to do? I didn't want to go down on him because I knew the pain would radiate through me for days afterwards. I didn't want to play in the snow because the cold temperature would cause inexplicable pains that felt like needles were weaving through my neurons. Have I stopped going for runs because my mind is subservient to my body? Do I walk slower than everyone else because of an inherited weakness?

"Disability" was never a word I assigned to myself. I wasn't disabled. I rejected that term and clung desperately to the gilded lie of 'normal.'

Most people remarked on how thin and healthy I looked, unaware that I was underweight and often skipped meals either due to lack of finances, the excruciating pain in my jaw, or an anxiety that penetrated mind and body. I'd explain away people's looks of concern when I took stairs too slowly or declined playing any sport with, "Don't worry! I'm just an old soul trapped in a young body."

Massage was something my ex-family never discussed beyond the immediate dismissal, the same way they would describe gynecologists ("they're secretly perverts in disguise who want to see you naked"). This was one of their many paranoid tactics to isolate me from anyone: "don't ask too many questions in class, teachers don't want to hear your annoying voice—don't speak to counselors about what happens here, that's family business—don't linger after choir practice to talk, you're just wasting people's time when they want to rush home." The list was infinite, my loneliness more extensive.

Playtime was denied to me throughout childhood. Why would it be normal for a body to begin playing with such exuberance now that I was free? I wasn't allowed to play outside unless supervised. Even as a teenager, at the grocery store, I was never allowed to wander down an aisle by myself—I was required to stay mere feet away from them to ensure I wasn't kidnapped; I wasn't allowed to answer the door for anyone, not even for grandparents; I was never allowed to cross the street to check the mail; I was never allowed to visit friends' houses nor go on field trips that weren't supervised by my mother. I wasn't allowed to have friends. As long as my memory lasts, my mother never had friends and she wasn't allowed to drive or go to work until I was in middle school. Her husband, my father, had complete control over all of us.

Even limited freedom wasn't without restraint. If mom spoke to anyone when she came out of the brick building from work, none of us would hear the end of it for a week; if she was found speaking to a man, she would suffer the repercussions for weeks. Eventually she was trained to ensure that she was the first out of the door, lips sealed tightly, her jawline quivering with buried emotion.

It was from my mother that I first heard of TMJ(D); she explained that it was like having arthritis in the jaw. Whenever I tried to touch her face as a young child, she would smack my hand away. She refused to ride certain roller coasters, claiming the ride was too jarring and too bumpy for her jaw to handle. Sometimes she'd talk about the good ol' days, before she had pain in her jaw, how she ate jawbreaker candy and never had to think about what it was like to have a broken jaw.

I inherited my mother's jaw. Our jaws were whittled away over a generation's shame. My mother blamed my birth for her reason to stay with an abusive man. I thus bore the double weight from both of their abuse.

Yet, this masseuse's hands eased tension which had coagulated over twenty years; this woman I had met for the first time touched me with more love than my mother ever held me with. I hadn't told the masseuse about my own experiences, but in an instant, she knew about my (previous and ongoing) trauma just by noticing the patterns in my body. Did she guess that I have complex PTSD that releases via panic attacks when my feet are touched? Did she know based on the way my shoulders slumped inwards toward my body? Did she guess from the quiet timbre of my voice? Or did she possess an uncanny insight that allowed her to know that I ran away from my abusive family after I turned eighteen? My questions collected until I fell into silence as she kneaded the knots in my body into smaller concentrations of pain.

When she reached my lower back, I plucked up the courage to speak. Do people normally talk during massages, I wondered? "So, my friends and I have been disagreeing about what these are." I reached around and tapped one of the twin fist-sized knots in my lower back. "I'm pretty sure they're knots but two of my guy friends say it's ridiculous. They said it's definitely bone. But I'm not really sure." I bit my lip. "Can you tell?"

"Well, I can tell you that women most certainly don't have bones in this part of their body. And I presume this, like in your neck, has a radiating pain when you press it?"

"Mm, yes."

"Bones also don't do that. You were right."

I exhaled, considering the implications. I wasn't crazy; I was right about the composition of my body. On the other hand... "Is that really bad? Why are they there?" I reabsorbed her words from earlier, considering how the tension in my neck affects everything else in my body.

"It's never a good thing to be in pain. At the size that they are now, it would be ideal if you could receive a massage weekly for two years. That would cure your condition. But if it's left to grow, it may cause additional pain, potential numbing, and impaired mobility."

I closed my eyes as the tinkling rainforest music and her cordial ironing around the epicenter of my knots released pins and needles through my legs.

I never knew what it was like to play as a child. On annual summer vacations to the beach and anytime we were allowed outside: oh, how we were screamed at not to run (we might cut our feet in the sand, we might trip down the sand dune and break our neck, or we might be kidnapped if we ran out of sight).

I was so certain that I would be yelled at on the playground at school, even away from my parents' hateful gaze, that I often hid a book in my clothing and crawled to some corner or forsaken slide to read. On days my teachers scolded me and made me return a book to my desk, I'd instead plunge into the realm of my imagination: I drafted daydream friends and eventually original characters to fly across the playground. Running and flying were equally inaccessible to me; what difference would it make if I could bestow both gifts to fictional characters?

On the massage table, I closed my eyes, not willing to entertain tears. I thought of the Chinese idiom: 整体观念.[9] We must understand the

---

[9] Zhěngtǐ guānniàn

situation by considering it as an entity; regarding Chinese medicine, the body cannot be isolated from a part. The mind, the body, the limitations, and the fears—they are all integrated.

After the massage, I thanked her profusely. While the concept of being able to erase my lower back knots and their debilitating pain seemed miraculous, I knew that I couldn't afford weekly massages.

When my classmate in Xi'an told me it was normal to tip after a massage in the US, I gripped the inside of my wrist, half-crescents not painful enough to alleviate my shame. The masseuse in Kenosha had treated me with such dignity, shared generous insight, and treated me with compassion. And I had left without tipping. In that moment, I determined that I would select a special gift from the art street outside Beilin, Xi'an and book a massage once I returned and give her a double tip. Alas, when I returned my senior year, the cafe-joint-massage shop had closed permanently. I've never been able to repay her kindness.

After the massage with Xie Shīfù, he invites me to sit for a while. I step gingerly from the massage table, relishing the expanded sensation in my body from the release. He offers a cup of 补养.[10] tea—a concoction of goji berries, dates, and other plants that have been steeping all morning. He asks how long I have been vegetarian, and I am again rendered speechless. How does he know?

He inclines his head in encouragement for me to drink the warm beverage, revealing that he too is a vegetarian and Buddhist. Our *yuánfēn*. The cup warms the tips of my fingers and as I sip, warmth spreads throughout my body. He advises me to avoid eating ice cream, green tea, and fruits during winter. He suggests that if I am so inclined to eat fruit this season, then I must first soak them in boiled water. "*Only drink boiled water or bǔyǎng tea after massages, and never drink cold water or*

---

[10] Bǔyǎng. *Yang enhancing or warming.*

green tea." His voice carries a note of devotion—one of fatherly concern. It is a loving tenor, the kind that I've learned only strangers can bestow.

I press a lock of hair out of my face and consider the Chinese idiom: 牵一发而动全身.[11] To move a single strand of hair is to affect the entire body.

---

[11] Qiān yī fà ér dòng quánshēn

Kimberly Jae

The Beginning of a Long Poem on Why I Burned the Hospital Down

After Lawrence Benford

The doctors celebrated
Through my worsening illness
Babbling in blood tests, CT scans
Pulsing through my veins
This sun shone darkness
where light should have landed
Carved contempt instead of diagnosis
Mental illness instead of Lupus

Out of the corners of my consciousness
Only spot free of clutter and wayward shocks
Shined on broken pieces of blood clots
Drifted down through my arteries and veins
Searching for a spot to stop the blood
To stop consciousness

This hospital
Stocked full of deafening, deadly arrogance
Black bodies too young and subhuman to be broken
Medical care rationed for those white enough to wipe the slate clean

These hands
Built societies
now pray for societies
to not prey on them
To pray for them

These brain cells
Bursts of brilliance
Sparks electrical shocks
Burst into flames
So now I spit fire
My face melts into frozen drooped half smiles
This Black Womyn not allowed to feel pain as others do
For my right-side to whither as this building burns
As holes meant to dispense cure are plugged with silence, contempt,
    and GASOLINE
I burn as much as this hospital does

My body
Soulless
Forced to wither
AS THE FLAME CONSUMES ILLNESS,
I WAS TOLD
WAS IN MY HEAD

Trusting in modern medical marvels not available to the bodies tortured
to develop THEM
I watch this motherfucker burn
This heat
EVAPORATES TEARS NEVER ALLOWED TO FALL
This wind
Carries this flame through abandoned houses
Other structures we were never meant to be
While beating the broken and bloody
They allow insurrection
Spread rebellion throughout the wretched
Before gentrification kills us all

They decide to let nature take its course
And this hospital
Outstretches its arms
TO KEEP US OUT

In a second,
I am to be lynched
Watch the flames burn this space that wouldn't've allowed me in anyway
FLICKER
Then watch my skin pool into helplessness
My bones powder into dust
But still be the beast I am accused of being
I still hurt under the bravado and gasoline
I still swing from this noose and tree
As I will watch this motherfucker burn

As they sleep soundly in warmth
That their lullabied screams & melted bodies
POOLED WITH OUR ASHES AND
BAD MEDICAL ADVICE
PROVIDE

Duane L. Herrmann

Cooking Lesson

"Don't go near the stove!"
became:
stand beside the flames –
but be careful!
In terror,
eye-level flames,
I objected.
Overruled:
"Stir."
"But I can't see."
"Stir!"
Over my head,
spoon at awkward angle,
I stirred I knew not what.
Back and forth, round and round.
Short years later
I cooked entire meals
alone.

Cynthia Romanowski

Wrestle Mania

It starts with something happening. Maybe a death in the family. Maybe a fight with your husband or wife or child. It's in the way a stranger looks at you. The way that little things are off. The way your rearview mirror is tilted dramatically to the left and you don't remember tilting it. The way that small objects, stuff that you always always always keep in the same place, turn up elsewhere or don't turn up at all. It's when you make up reasons for all these things. When your mind races through dozens of possibilities until it completely forgets what the thing was in the first place, and you try to keep track so you can explain it all to someone, but you can't keep track. Can't keep a thought for six seconds. Write single words down but forget. It's when cars start to honk rudely because you're going thirty-five miles per hour on the freeway, and you didn't even realize you were on the freeway. And now that you realize it you've completely forgotten where you're going. What you did yesterday. What you did five minutes ago. Your hands shake and you wonder whether they are shaking because it's happening again or if it's nerves. Maybe what's happening is just nerves. Maybe it's just too much caffeine. Maybe a beer will mellow you out. Maybe you're just flighty and distracted like your mother. Maybe that lyric on the radio that you turned to *precisely* the same *moment* when she called didn't mean anything. Does she really call that often? Didn't it ring once before she hung up? Or was it a blocked number? Didn't it ring? It's when you can't walk normally, or you can but it's weird to walk because people are looking and, in your head, you're saying I'm walking normal. Stop walking weird! Why are you walking weird? Walk normal! And you can't remember if you said that out loud and now you have to get away from people. From music. From cars. Synchronicity. The talk back:

Why am I so sensitive?

Why are you?

I'm too sensitive.

You've just tuned in again, that's all.

I'm fine.

You are fine.

I'm gonna be fine.

The magical thinking starts but you know better. Know that it's impossible to intuit other people's thoughts. Impossible to have a headache because the whole world is hurting and you're a vessel. But you can't not believe and believing changes all. Reasons, secrets, theories. Pop, pop, popping in your head. All answers. To all mysteries. This, because this, because this, which is exactly the same as that. That which just happened, what was that thing? And it's impossible to ignore just how *perfectly* each fucking thing/thought/answer feels just undeniably, certainly, *positively* like someone else has placed it there. Because someone else has placed it there. You find a piece of paper with the word "mirror" written in your handwriting. You didn't write that. Who does that? Maybe it's a clue. So you rush to find your reflection. You, staring back at you. Staring back.

C.M. *Crockford*

Autistic's Scattered Song

neurotypicals, natural liars all//spit flies off wagging tongues//but they can't say a word//salesman sans a good pitch//rutting in your arms i hope you're real enough//or nothing is//when i was young sister sheltered while dad threw things and howled//(so I was told)//i never came out of hiding see//i was good//a great magician never reveals his secrets// especially with you//never with them never again//wear a mask// keep off the grass//control yourself//stop dancing//rules built before living memory//they were never worthy of me//but nothing really is//there is no one behind this curtain//i could eat this world and spit out the bones

Teresa Milbrodt

Cyclops Notes

The optometrist's assistant is impressed that I know the name of my eye condition. I wonder how I could not know it since I've had a long time to learn, but she says most people just describe the problem they're having with their vision—black specks or floaters or fuzzy traffic signs. My sight has always been a problem, but if something is a problem long enough you stop thinking of it as a problem because it's simply what is. I have a hard time holding my eye open in bright light, so when the optometrist's assistant takes laser pictures, my lower eyelid keeps getting in the way. On her computer screen, my eye looks like a waning moon.

*

When I was a kid, the fact I was blind in one eye was kind of cool. It made me different. It made me special. It was something I could tell other kids at school: *Hey, I'm blind in one eye.* But this revelation led to the inevitable test. The kid I'd told would hold up their hand in front of my right eye and say, "How many fingers am I holding up?"

"I don't know," I'd say, "it's blind."

Even when I was eight, I didn't understand their logic. If my eye weren't blind, I could've lied and told them the wrong number. Other kids didn't notice the blindness so much as the fact I held books closely when I read. I also needed glasses to see things that were far away, and to protect my sighted eye. That was something my mother and Dr. Neville, my ophthalmologist, drilled into my head from a young age: No contacts. Ever. The glasses were important to improve the vision in my sighted eye, but they also protected both eyes from pens or pencils or strange bits of flying debris that I might not see in time to blink. My glasses, my shields.

*

This is retinopathy of prematurity: When a baby is born early, at thirty-one weeks gestation or less, the blood cells in their eyes can grow abnormally, toward the center of the eye instead of around the retina, which makes the retina detach.[1] A baby's eyes develop the most during the last three months before birth, time I didn't have. Cells are less likely to cooperate if you want to get out early. (My mother says I have always been impatient to get things done.) I had an operation on my right eye when I was four and a half months old to try to save my sight. It didn't work.

Que verra verra. What will see will see.

Retinopathy of prematurity is much less common now than it was in years past since doctors understand how to monitor oxygen levels more carefully and decrease the likelihood that a premature infant will have retinal detachment. When I was born, they knew just enough about how to keep preemies my size alive past the most critical period. Other babies in my NICU may have had more severe vision problems later in life, and about half of them didn't make it.

When I explain this to people, I end with a shrug and say "Yeah, so I'm just happy to be here."

*

I'm disabled and not. To me my eye isn't really a disability because I've

---

[1] "Retinopathy of Prematurity." *National Eye Institute*, Department of Health and Human Services, National Institutes of Health, June 2014, https://www.nei.nih.gov/learn-about-eye-health/eye-conditions-and-diseases/retinopathy-prematurity

always had it, and "disability" suggests a more severe limitation, some adjustment you have to make partway through life. What I have is a way of living. I must be careful on stairs, and when descending rocky slopes on hikes. I position myself at the far-right corner of the table when I go out to eat with a group of people, and when walking with friends I stay on their right, so they don't get lost in my empty space. These are things I do automatically. I am also awful at sports that involve catching or throwing or kicking a ball. This could be because I have no depth perception. It could also be because I am awful at sports.

*

I'm accustomed to the rituals of eye appointments, to people shining bright lights in my face and telling me to look up, right, down, left. I like this new optometrist, who's pleased to learn that my research involves disability studies. I explain that when you have a blind eye, it's hard not to be drawn to that field. Some part of me has always recognized that I see things differently than most people. He says the things that happen to us in life often drive our interests. "Mine, too," he adds, then explains he was a preemie and has a lazy eye because of it. It wasn't retinopathy of prematurity—I have to ask that question—but his eye didn't develop as it should. One day when he was six or seven, he discovered he could read much better if he covered one eye. He asked his mom if it was supposed to work that way. After that he started therapy to strengthen the lazy eye, so now both his eyes track together. I envy the fact they can agree on one direction, but, essentially, he is a person like me, half-sighted. That's part of the reason why he decided to go into medicine.

"I tried working in a hospital during my undergraduate years, but it was too intense," he says. "I feel too much for other people." Empathy. I can understand that.

"How big were you?" he asks.

"Twenty-four weeks. Two pounds, thirteen ounces," I say.

"You were smaller than me," he says, but they are saving babies at twenty-one weeks now and know how to treat retinopathy of prematurity more effectively than when we were born, by monitoring oxygen levels. A few decades ago, doctors hadn't realized that higher oxygen levels put babies at higher risk for retinopathy. But now more preemies grow up to have retinal detachment in later life, losing their sight in their twenties and thirties. My fear of delayed retinopathy was why I made this eye appointment.

Everyone has their own version of "people like us," the insider conversations you can have with folks who are otherwise strangers. This is one of mine.

*

I function as a sighted person, but my feet are on the edge of that world. I know how simple it would be to slide into sightlessness and need to learn braille, get adaptive texts and a cane, and re-learn how to cook. But total blindness is something I consider in an abstract way, like how someday I'll probably have arthritis, but until my knees and fingers start aching it's just a theory.

Often, my friends don't know that I'm blind in my right eye. Some have mentioned that they noticed my right eye doesn't track along with the left, but they assume it's a lazy eye and don't think much of it. I don't think much of it most of the time, until I bump into someone at the grocery store or slam someone's hand in a freezer door.

*

Because the laser pictures aren't as clear as he'd like, the optometrist asks if I would mind if he dilated my eyes. I say that's fine. He says we'll both feel better. I agree. I say I'm accustomed to the sting of dilation drops, but he may need to hold my eye open to get them in. Dr. Neville always did.

"You did fine," he says, after adding drops to the left eye.

"You didn't know me when I was six," I say.

He says that when he was in school, the optometry students would practice giving each other dilation drops and shining lights in their eyes after class.

"If you think this is bad," he says, "you should try it with someone who's just learning how to do it."

*

Our shared space was the space of laughter, me and my new optometrist. This is how I explain the benefits of my blind eye: It's a useful place to hide things I don't want to look at, when I don't want to reveal that I'm not looking. What you can't see can't hurt you. Except when it can.

Perhaps I do this too much, make light of my half-blindness, twist it into a joke since I can't do anything else. Humor is a kind of bleak acceptance, as laughter often cloaks something deeper. A fear. An anxiety. That which cannot be spoken except through a joke, a smirk, a casual shrug. But does that mean we are hiding in darkness, hiding from darkness, or just molding it into something we can look at without wincing?

*

When I was a year old, my parents tried to make me wear a prosthesis, a plastic eye cover that was supposed to fit over my blind eye like a little cap. Mom kept it in my baby book along with hair from my first haircut. The prosthesis is in a small plastic bag sticking out between the pages inscribed with my birth weight and length. The eye looks like half a marble hollowed out, like something that was popped out of a doll's head. It was supposed to slide into my eye socket, and my ophthalmologist at the time wanted me to wear it since my body was still developing.

"She was concerned the bones around your eye wouldn't grow properly and you would have a space that wasn't symmetrical," my mom says.

But I couldn't wear the prosthesis without it bothering me.

"It was terrible for us, too," says Mom, since my parents had to hold me down on the couch to slip it on. "It was like a little torture every day."

"I don't think it took very long and we gave up," says my dad. That story had a happy ending since everything developed as it should, aside from the fact that my blind eye is a little smaller than the sighted one. I can't blame my infant self for throwing a tantrum, because the eye cover looks more like a toddler torture device than anything helpful. Whoever invented it probably didn't have kids.

*

During my yearly exam, Dr. Neville had to put stinging drops in my eyes to dilate the pupils so he could examine my retinas. When I was little—four and five and six years old—I screamed and kicked and cried so much his assistant or my parents had to hold my arms and legs. When I was twenty-nine, we had the annual ritual of recounting how badly I'd reacted to eye drops when I was a kid, and how nice it was that I didn't do that anymore. Dr. Neville was my ophthalmologist for almost thirty years, so he memorized the retinal scarring in my left eye and drew it in my charts to make sure it didn't change. He also suggested a slight magnification on the right lens of my glasses so my blind eye would look the same size as my sighted one.

*

My mom says she thought about my half-blindness more often when I was younger, careening around the neighborhood on my bike and forgetting all the things I couldn't see.

"When we'd go to the playground, I'd worry that you would get hit with a swing or something because you wouldn't see from that side of your face and somebody would crash into you," Mom says, "or you'd crash into something. And always the concern that it would be awful if something happened to your other eye. I remember being happy when you got solid glasses."

I was four years old. They had ugly brown plastic frames.

"It was as soon as you were old enough to keep them on," says my dad, though I only wore them when I needed to see something at a distance. I forgot the glasses when we went to a Care Bears movie when I was six—I remember being upset that everything was blurry—but I started wearing them all the time when I was in first grade and could pick out the frame color (red) on my own.

*

People look cuter with glasses. Yes, I'm biased, but all kinds of things shape taste.

*

It's difficult to determine how growing up with a blind eye might have affected my personality, what experiences I would have gained or lost if I'd been fully sighted. Would I have been less empathetic, more extroverted, peered at myself for five seconds less in the mirror every day, and gone out for the junior high girls' basketball team? Would I have been less aware of the fragility of bodies and my own fragility, how people are always adaptable, but how adaptation takes time?

*

The nice thing about a visible disability is that people can see the wheelchair or white cane. They can ask if you need help. This is kind when it's not condescending, though it's amazing how quickly things can change from one to the other, how politeness can become overly parental when people assume disability means fragility. But when you shut someone's hand in a freezer door by mistake, you wish it were a little easier for other people to see that you can't see.

*

I think about positioning so much that I don't think about it—seating myself at the far-right corner when out to dinner with family and friends, sitting near the front of classrooms, walking on my friends' right sides. Sometimes in crowds the blind eye isn't that noticeable since everyone is bumping into everyone else, the space inevitably awkward and tight.

*

At a Halloween-themed reading in a dim bar, I step onstage to perform my work. The violet-hued spotlight is too dim, or the words on my page are too tiny, because the sentences become a blur. I stumble through the first few lines, then take off my glasses and hold the book a few inches from my face, at a low angle so I can see the print but not have my voice muffled behind the page. It feels and probably looks odd, so I try to compensate through volume and exuberance, my voice booming to the back of the room. The story is funny, and everyone has been drinking, so they laugh with me, which is better than the alternative. I close the book and slip my glasses back on. Applause. I bow and return to my seat, feeling awkward, awkward, awkward. My friends say I did well, and don't mention the glasses removal. Next time I'll bring a flashlight. I tell myself there's nothing wrong with needing adaptive devices.

*

When I walk somewhere with my friend Drew, who uses a wheelchair, he rolls across the street with a wave to any drivers saying, "They won't hit the crippled kid."

I say, "Yeah, but they will hit the half-blind girl who they don't realize is half-blind."

*

I wait for my eye to dilate. You can't do much as the world steadily blurs. I text my parents:

Me: *At the optometrist. He also has eye problems and was a preemie :) Getting dilated.*

After my appointment, I find a note from my dad: *Is this a routine check-up?*

I wonder what he imagined. Parents can dream anything.

*

Learning how to drive was interesting. I was behind the wheel of my mom's old minivan, and, according to her, I almost took out a few mailboxes until I learned that I should not center my vision in the middle of the road. Mostly I remember her gasping in the front passenger seat and being glad that I couldn't see her grip on the dashboard. My dad was a better driving instructor, or at least he was calmer. When we bumped over a curb, he told me not to take the turn as sharply the next time.

But even now I don't like driving in traffic or large cities. I'm not sure who I won't see, or who might not see me not seeing them. I'd rather walk, and look both ways, and look both ways again.

*

I say that I don't think about my blind eye much, that it doesn't really matter, but perhaps this is changing. I'm reading more, underlining, making margin notes, and must take off my glasses more often because peering through the bottom of the lens doesn't work well.

This is why people have bifocals when they're older, I think.

I don't get eyestrain or headaches from reading. Yet. Maybe this has been my blind spot, and disability will start to matter more. I will adjust, recalibrate, remind myself to look up from the page and blink. My normal may shift in tiny increments of stronger prescriptions. When I consider loss in that way it's bearable, like the slow accumulation of gray hairs and the way joints pop in the morning when you get out of bed. The body always gives signals, sign posts. We just choose to ignore them.

*

Once I was bumped by a minivan while crossing the street. I was living in Arlington, Virginia that summer, taking a morning walk before I went into my internship in Washington, DC. It was a light tap on my hip and the driver braked, but I went down on the pavement, an involuntary action as I thought *I have just been hit by a vehicle. That means I should fall.*

A young woman bulleted out of the driver's seat and said something along the lines of, "Oh my God, are you okay?"

"Yeah," I said, "it was just a bump on my hip. I'll be fine."

"But I hit you with my car," she said.

I spent the next five minutes trying to comfort her. She had two little kids strapped in car seats in the back of the minivan.

"Really, it's okay," I said, "I'm fine." My hip smarted a little.

"But I hit you with my car," she said again.

I said it was more of a tap, but she made me come home with her and asked if I wanted to go to the hospital. I said I was fine and called my boss at the internship to explain I'd had a problem and would be a little late to work. I don't think I said I was hit by a car. I might have said I was bumped by a car. I didn't want her to worry.

The young mother was far more shaken than me, fretting over how much worse I could have been injured. My Midwestern instinct was to remind her that I wasn't hurt too badly; I might just have a little bruise. I could walk back to my apartment on my own. She made me exchange contact information with her anyway, in case some injury surfaced, and I needed treatment.

I felt bad about being late to work—I was twenty-two and it was my first job that felt like a real one—but yes, I was reminded of how easy it was not to see. Now I wonder if that lady thought of me and looked once, twice, three times for pedestrians before turning. I wonder if she thought of me when teaching her own kids how to drive: *Remember that time, with that girl, when you were very young?*

*

The verdict is in at the optometrist: I need a stronger prescription. The reading I'm doing in disability studies is further disabling me. I don't care that much, since I know I'll never get rid of the glasses, and a lens is a lens is a lens.

"Have you ever seen pictures of your eye?" my optometrist asks when we're done with the exam. I shake my head. No one has ever offered before.

On his computer monitor, my left eye looks like the inside of an egg before the embryo has formed. There's a tangle of mostly well-behaved blood vessels and a macula that the optometrist says looks "beautiful." He points to scarring on one side of my retina, but says he's not worried about it. Mostly all quiet on the western front. I don't have late onset retinopathy. I'm just getting older.

Before I leave, he gives me the usual caution. Before he gives me the usual caution, he says he's sure I've heard the usual caution many times. If I ever notice anything is wrong with my vision, I need to call the office right away and not sleep on it.

I say I will do that, and I will see him in a year. I admit I should have been here earlier, but there was a lot going on with school, and it's annoying to establish yourself with a new doctor, to tell all the stories you tell to explain yourself and your problems.

He says he understands.

*

Maybe it was my friend Drew who started it by making me part of his in-group, on the list of people who "get it" and are thus privy to the details of catheter use and bowel obstruction. He remembers that I have a side he should be on. I remember that any time we go out for coffee, he'll need to use the bathroom three times because of his tiny bladder. We take turns opening the door for each other. In too many conversations, he'll mention beating the shit out of someone in a mosh pit, and the likelihood of dying from a kidney infection caused by a UTI.

Perhaps this is to say there are things about me that my disabled friends realize but my family doesn't. I can't understand everything about my friends' lives—if I careened around the world in a wheelchair for a day or a week or a month, I would not know what it is to be Drew—but even in that space of knowing that our experiences can't be simulated, we understand something important about each other.

When my mom had cataract surgery a few years ago, she drove home with one eye covered and no depth perception. Later, she said she thought of me on that drive, since it was how I always perceived the world.

"Well, kind of," I said, touched at the mention but wondering how close she could come to my perspective, which might be more or less disorienting since it's a what-has-always-been.

Maybe my mom knew that, but because she's a mother she has to do what she can.

*

This is one time when the right eye mattered: I was getting milk from a cooler in the college cafeteria and shut the door, then heard a loud "Ouch" on my right. I'd pinched the fingers of an invisible girl next to me who'd been reaching for juice, but I only saw her when I turned my head.

"You slammed the door on my hand," she said, glaring at me.

I realize that I must have seemed like a malicious bitch.

"I'm sorry," I said and tried to explain what didn't seem logical, that I hadn't seen her.

"My hand was right there," she said.

I told her I was blind in my right eye, that I really hadn't seen her. I felt like shit. She wasn't soothed. She shouldn't have been soothed because her hand still hurt like hell.

I might have followed her to the cashier, still apologizing. She might have said it was okay in a hard tone that suggested the opposite. I don't remember, but I hope I apologized until it got annoying. I hope she thought I sounded sincere.

*

I don't mean to pass as fully sighted. Perhaps I should wear a pirate eye patch, making the invisible visible, perhaps assuring that even I would remember my difference during the twenty-three hours and fifty minutes of every day (on average) when my disability does not matter, and the ten minutes when the sighted and non-sighted worlds collide. Often, I forget I am in both of them.

*

Two days after Thanksgiving. I was driving across town on Main Street, a tricky road with four narrow lanes and cars parallel parked on either side. I was in the rightmost lane and don't remember the sound exactly, but it must have been a scrape, and probably a thud. Something had happened. I decided it would be wise to stop, so I pulled over at the crosswalk and put on the hazard lights. Behind me was a white car and a gray-haired lady. The rear passenger door on the driver's side of her car was bent back toward the hood. She'd been getting out when I came along and clipped the edge of her door. I slid out of the van apologizing, and she started yelling that I'd almost killed her.

"You weren't paying attention," she said. "Were you listening to music?"

I said I was sorry, very sorry, that I was blind in my right eye, and I hadn't seen the car door.

"You're blind in your right eye?" she said. "Why are you even driving?"

I kept babbling I'm sorry, I'm sorry, I'm sorry, because I was just eighteen and hadn't had a license for that long. I'm not sure in what order everything happened, but someone called the police, and I found the insurance card and registration information in the glove compartment and was crying on the sidewalk when I felt a hand on my shoulder. A brown-haired lady who looked to be my mom's age said, "Teresa, I don't know if you remember me, but I'm Mrs. Vollmar. I was your elementary school nurse."

She hugged me like a mother, and lent me her (big, blocky) cell phone so I could call my mom and explain the accident. Mrs. Vollmar hugged me again after I called my mom, while I told the police officer what had happened. The screaming lady yelled at the police officer, saying I should be cited and why was I even allowed to drive and I could have killed her.

After my mom arrived, I huddled with her and Mrs. Vollmar on the sidewalk, shaking. I never wanted to drive again. It was cold and gray, a typical Midwestern November afternoon, though the lampposts on Main would have been wrapped with tinsel by then and hung with those big green wreaths like life preservers.

When I ask her about the accident, my mother mostly recalls her anger at the screaming lady.

"She kept blaming you and it was all her fault," Mom says. "I remember standing on the sidewalk talking to her. I remember you tearing up and being very apologetic and her being a jerk. Initially I thought she was like a vulture. 'Your insurance will pay for this!' She was awful."

It was the first time I heard my mother use the word "bitch" to refer to anyone, but that was later when we were driving home with her behind the wheel.

"I remember being impressed at that," I say.

"I remember saying that," says my mother.

The police officer was kind and told the screaming lady that I could not be cited because her car door was over the white parking line. If anyone might be cited, he said, it was her. Our van was scraped along the side, but drivable. Her car was not. My dad says our insurance companies negotiated and ended up splitting the repair bill.

It's only now that I let myself be angry. The passage of time means I can stand on the sidewalk in my memory, an almost-observer as I watch her yell at my young self. An older me demands answers from the yelling lady: Why didn't you look for oncoming traffic before you opened the door? Whose blind spot was really at fault? Why couldn't you accept my fifth "I'm sorry" and quit haranguing me since I felt guilty enough? How much more remorse did you think you could squeeze out of an eighteen-year-old kid?

In my hands-on-hips self-righteousness, I confront her with the same indignation my mother seethed, but some of it is borrowed emotion, permission to be angry that has been granted to me because Mom is still upset when she recalls the incident.

I also know the screaming lady is right. Whoever's fault the accident was, I could have killed or seriously injured her.

*

I don't remember which side the van tapped me on, right or left, and I don't know why that has been erased from my memory. I remember the young mother had two kids in the back seat. I remember she was far more shaken than I was. I remember rubbing my hip and standing in the hallway of her tidy house as she asked me five times if I was sure, really sure, that I didn't want to go to the hospital. I can't remember who didn't see who. Does it matter?

*

A friend once asked me if I would have the vision restored in my right eye if I could. I said I didn't think that was possible. Even if my retina could be reattached, my brain isn't accustomed to receiving signals from that eye and wouldn't know what to make of them. My friend had more faith in my brain's plasticity and repeated the question. I thought for a moment and said no. I wouldn't have restorative surgery.

But why stay with what I have? Because it is familiar? Because it makes me different? Because I would lose my ability to strategically hide things in my empty space? Because I have spent the past thirty-odd years negotiating the world with one eye and it's worked well enough, thank you very much, so there's no reason to change and admit that things could have been better, or perhaps just different, if I had two sighted eyes? Because everyone tends to assume that wholeness, or our definition of it, is always better than partial, but I'm not ready to make that assumption?

*

Life means continually revising what is normal, embracing your tenuousness, wondering if the twinge in your elbow is temporary or permanent. Nobody is ever out of the woods. Life is all about the woods. Like a fish isn't conscious of water, we're not conscious of the woods until we bump into a tree, or graze past it close enough to feel the bark, then we look up and see the woods. We hurt, we mend, we adapt, we get back to something called normal. We resume ignoring the woods.

*

Mom: *How was your examination?*
  Me: *I need a stronger script*
  Mom: *Wow, the first time in years for a script change. Very much change?*
  Me: *Yes*
  Mom: *Affecting distance or close up vision or both?*
  Me: *Distance*
  Mom: *Dad said that happened to him at the same age*
  Me: *I have a beautiful macula, though*
  Mom: *Dad said "Well, that's good." (Smile)*
  I smile, too, close my phone, and think, *Well. Something hereditary.*

Laura Mulqueen

800-273-TALK

I called the helpline
again last night, made
agreements I don't know
if I can keep.
How from one room
do I slip
right into others:
downtown alleys, beds
I drowned in,
the need to evaporate?
When I become solid,

I'll be the voice on the other
end of the line—the one who
assures without knowing
when, or if, landfall will come,
the one who sails you safely
through another nightfall
into morning.

Zackary Medlin

Bipolar II

I want to tell you something important today,
like, "if we just stand here hard enough at dawn,
the sun will break like an egg & all that yellow
will finally bind us together. We'll all rise, be
leavened to heaven by this, our recipe of hours
that bakes into something bright & sweet,
a lemon cake, maybe." I want to tell you another
definition of leaven is "to permeate & transform
something for the better." I want to eat my cake,
too, but I can't stomach that saccharine shit.

The pills do help. So I take my Lamictal,
my Wellbutrin, but my brain sometimes
still only wants for me to want to die.
Please don't ask what's wrong; it's nothing.
Nothing is wrong, except all my favorite songs
have gone ghost, grown emptier at every chorus,
sang away their insides, hollowed themselves
into echoes that hurt to hear. So I'm left
sitting cold, flipping through a crate of records,
a head full of photographs, while my pulse slows
to the frequency of yearning needed to burn
everything to feel just a bit warmer, then wash
in the ash of all the gone things. I want to tell you

something insignificant, complain about traffic,
ask how your day went, but the best I can do is get
under a blanket in a bed I've forgotten how to use.
When you lay beside me, you'll brush your fingers
against all the nights I didn't die. You'll whisper to me:
"Goodnight. Sleep well." Maybe I will, but all I can say
with any certainty is: "I'll see you in the morning."

Latif Askia Ba

Houses

Even houses are strange.
They live in you.
They're shaped of corners and doorways,
parts of apartments and crammed lodgings—
private as a pair of testicles.

Houses cut you open:
a jagged wood,
a very bad word,
a question.

Aren't all houses questions?
A moth coming to dismantle you:
she sets the parts down carefully.

The sun is out anyway:
like a light, like a baby.
There is pitchness in a bedroom
before there is darkness—
like dancing before there is talking,
like this song that has befallen me:

A scale chips off an ancient angelic tile.
A toe cuts on the chipped tile.
A cry in the bath.

A chipped cup, a loose stair,
a stain on the thinnest carpet.
A fireplace suffocated by shelves of unread books
like ancient specimens, some worn through,
the words half-erased: their soot encases
their rotten leaves.

Houses like the warmth of a god or the bite of a devil,
Dostoyevsky's toothache, Lao Tsu's cup of water,
the Buddha's bowl of rice, Camus' sun.

Houses drowned in time. Years flood
and fling open doors and windows;
years scrape the wood floors white;
minutes stick to surfaces like bacterial colonies;
seconds stick to coats like glitter.

Houses like bombs ticking away
in a refrigerator drawer—
too cold to detonate—they die
like people do: slowly or taken by a tropical gust,
they tear from the ground like splinters from a finger,
they tangle themselves in the chambers of the mind,
folded and tucked in a nook of gray matter—
an intimate closet
with an old glass knob and warped threshold;
a closet guests have no reason to open.

And the wardrobe, in its generosity, leaves an inheritance:
a dying washing machine, a garden devoured by winter,
an old CPU, a bird unnamed by man.

Myths of Inheritance: Cardamom

My mother's life, her dad before her, all of us since; we all hinge on that one moment. My great-grandmother took her first breath.

But, I am moving too fast. Try again.

Remember this.

My mom's Oma, on her father's side. Sigridur "Sigga" Matheldur Danielson was born on Hecla Island, New Iceland. The island is a park now, but the house has been preserved. You can take a tour. You can see the stove and oven, assorted furniture. Actually, I am not sure what you can see. I've never been there. What I do know is that on January 13, 1912, Sigga, my Sigga, was born into this world. I like to think she slipped in between the folds.

I imagine her mother, my great-great-grandmother, Gundrun Vilhelmina "Mina" Danielson, born Helgadottir in Mikley, Manitoba, married in Bifrost, living on Hecla, tending the tasks of everyday survival, the softening round of her belly beneath layers of clothing and the cold of January. I imagine a small pinch in her back, the left side, as she reached toward the teats to massage the udder of the goat I imagine she kept. Mina always warmed her hands, but never quite enough. I imagine the bleat of the goat, the turn of its head in pretend startle. I imagine her sitting at the milking stool. I imagine the warm smell of goat and grasses tamped and broken, lifted and stirred. I imagine the metallic thrust of the wind and its near-invisible shards of ice cutting in from the northeast. I imagine Mina never had time for nonsense, but that she took pleasure in curling her hair for a special occasion.

That January morning, I imagine the sun. Is it bright in Manitoba the way it is in Alberta? I imagine the rhythms of a farmhouse at waking, Mina, her husband, Leifi, the two of them each on their day underway, adjacent and allied. I imagine the kitchen in their home, the lingering smell of some roasted coffee. Mina takes the beans from a tin in the larder. I can see Mina reaching for one of the filters she'd sewn from her Leifi's old shirt, the blue flannel that just would not hold the seam any longer. Adding the coffee, the chickory, and just one small touch of kardemom. حَبُهان. I come by cardamom on both sides. I come by cardamom honestly. Although she woke feeling strange, I imagine Mina took care to make sure each cup matched its saucer. There is hard fish and bread on the table.

—Leifi, come. The coffee is warm.

I can see Mina take her coffee just so (clink glass)—*sykur og síðan krem*, sugar and then cream. A small quick swallow of bread and then the second beginning of the day with its layers and boots and chores. The faster done, the better. What a strange feeling. Upon entering the shed, a little past the ice house—that's on the website—I imagine Mina warming her hands with her mind somehow two steps behind her. And, as she reaches toward the goat and places her hands upon the warm and cold of that milk-heavy udder, I imagine her back.

I imagine her back.

I imagine her back.

—No, Leifi, it is too soon.

I imagine the blankets. I imagine the praying. I imagine the heat, impossible heat, a moist heat, the fires blazing, water warming. I imagine my great-great-grandfather tending his own helplessness by focusing on the task at hand, making of himself an industry of warming. I imagine him holding her as she reached for the impossible tremble that somehow slipped between the folds of her body, the bedding, this home.

—Oh, Leifi.

I imagine that no matter the date or time, the ashes and cinder it would be to bear a dead child. It is ashes and cinder to be in the what if. That space between breath in and breath out. It is our way, in this culture, to force past this moment. To breathe it out. To shake it off. But what, then, of the not enough? Does too much then become not enough? And what comes after? For me, it's the mourning—not the performance of grief, but the verb that works through a person, the verb that is rendered by a person, their hands, their heart. The way mouths move around stories. The imagination that rises to meet us at the door. That is griefwork. It takes the time and space it needs. It fills the time and space it is offered. It takes the time and space it takes. It surges and overflows. It falls in deep spiral and resurfaces at the oddest times. It is life and death and life again. It is death and life and death again. It is tender and cutting. It is the temperature of blood and fire. It is our work here. Good mourning.

How many mamadadabibibobobabas are in wait of mourning?

But, where were we then? Oh, yes. It is morning.

I imagine Mina entering the goat shed, taking hands out of her pockets, rubbing them for warmth to keep the shock off the goat, but somehow her mind, two steps behind, is thinking on the smell of kardemom. She pulls the stool and sits—oof just a small tug of the back, come on, Mina. She places the bucket beneath the warm and cold of one milk-heavy udder and sings. *Sofðu unga ástin mín* as she reaches toward the goat. *Úti regnið grætur*. Thoughts pulled through a foggy place, Mina shifts on the stool to account for her back *Mamma geymir gullin þín*, and places her hands against the stretch and full, as she does every morning, every evening, *gamla leggi og völuskrín*. Mina sings as she eases the goat's way of it. *Við skulum ekki vaka um dimmer nætur.*

She sings until the goat chews calm. *Það er margt sem myrkrið veit.* She sings and thinks upon her mother. *Minn er hugur þungur.* She sings to pull away from that spot in her back. *Oft ég svarta sandinn leit.* She sings to pass the time in the damp cold of this barn. *Svíða grænan engireit.* She pulls and rolls the teats from top to bottom and sets the milk to flow. *Í jöklinum hljóða dauðadjúpar sprungur.* It takes no imagination to consider the sound of milk against itself, *Sofðu lengi, sofðu rótt,* against the aluminum bucket. *Seint mun best að vakna.* No imagination to feel the tingle in Mina's feet as the edge of the stool costs the arteries of her thighs some of their circulation. *Mæðan kenna mun þér fljótt.* It is no effort to hear Mina's voice strain a little against the pinch-pull of her back. *Meðan hallar degi skjótt.* It is easy to feel the bellow of her lungs expand and compress a familiar rhythm, keeping time with the pull, with the sound of milk against itself, the overtone sung aluminum creeping higher and higher. *Að mennirnir elska, missa, gráta og sakna.* Slowly. Chord and discord. In and out. Press, pinch, pull, release.

I imagine her back.

I imagine her back.

I imagine her back.

—No, Leifi, it is too soon.

I imagine the blankets. I imagine the praying. I imagine the heat, impossible heat, a moist heat, the fires blazing, water warming. I imagine my great-great-grandfather tending his own helplessness by focusing on the task at hand, making of himself an industry of warming. I imagine him holding her as she reached for the impossible tremble that somehow slipped between the folds of her body, the bedding, this home.

—Oh, Leifi.

It is ashes and cinder to bear a dead child. *Sleep my little love. Look at it there. Outside the rain is weeping. So small. Mama keeps watch over your gold. I imagine tender hands. Old leg bones and a little treasure chest.* I imagine Mina drying the grey-dusk of her babe. *Let's not stay awake through dark nights. To hold and to look once, there is much that darkness knows, just once.* My mind is heavy. I imagine Mina drying the grey-dusk of her babe. *Often, I've seen the black sand,* to hold and to look once, *Scorching green meadows.* Just once. *In the glacier rumbles deadly-deep cracks.* It is ashes and cinder to bear a dead child. *Sleep long, sleep tight.* Look at it there. *It's best to wake up late.* So small. *Hardship will teach you soon.* I imagine her tender hands. *While the day becomes night.* To hold and to look once. Just once. *That the people love, lose, cry, and mourn.*

Tenderness, out of the hands of it, does not often translate. It does not pull across languages well, even if it does thread through them, especially in song—attempts to translate are either under-inflected or well overdrawn. There is no mother tongue for: We were wild once. We are born. We domesticate. We rewild. And then, if we are lucky, we die clear. Nothing stuck. How to tell the real of these things to you? How to share the shapes of Mina, of Leifi? The ashes and cinder of it all?

—No, Leifi, it is too soon.

Imagine, then, their surprise when that new babe gave a gurgle, and a gasp. Imagine it pinking a little at the chest. Imagine that babe widening its eyes, in horror, perhaps, in fear, as its body begins to pull through the sticky ropes of surfactant it was statistically improbable of having made. Imagine that babe, wide-eyed in surprise: lungs, throat, mouth, nose all full and blocked, that moment when what once knew only liquid would now take in air.

—Mina, Mina. Rub her again.

I imagine my great-great-grandmother, hands finding their authority fast, cradling the jaw, and flipping that babe, so the pull of the earth could offer its service to this precious and tender life. I imagine her rubbing, equal parts caution and vigor.

—No, Leifi, it is too soon.

But it takes no imagination at all to hear that first cry: not the mew of a kitten, nothing hesitant, nothing held in reserve. Smothered in the folds. On January 13, 1912, my great-grandmother, Sigridur Matheldur Danielson, announced her will to stay. I am told that she was born sixty-seven years, less a day, to me. I am told that she weighed exactly two pounds one ounce—me too, me too. I am told her tiny body was kept warm in a shoe box lined with blankets that sat on the open oven door—in a way, me too. I am told that my Sigga was fed milk through an eye dropper because she could not hold a swallowful without bringing it right back up—pyloric stenosis. I had it, too.

Two pounds, one ounce.

1912.

1979.

Remember this.

Small sips.

Speaking truthfully, I don't know if Leifi and Mina had goats. I do not know if they worked together. I do not know where my great-grandmother was born, or who was there. I do imagine great tenderness, because it serves me to imagine great tenderness. But, truthfully, the men all along that line of my family were as likely to be cold to their wives as they were to hold them. My family was poor. Winters are ice-dark frozen. A heart can be rendered threadbare in a thousand thousand ways.

When I think of Oma Sigga's birth, I usually think something like the one I wrote just now. But it is equally easy to imagine my great-great grandmother all alone in the house, labouring and terrified. It is easy to imagine the presence of a Prussian-trained midwife speaking little common language but making all the right sounds. It is easy to imagine her in a bed in Morden Hospital, ready for the Ordeal—but then, of course, that could not have been. At that time obstetrics was not in the business of preserving life, or, if that was its business, it was not very good at it. Born so small into the hands of a physician, transferred to the hands of a nurse to be cleaned, mother dizzy and feverish, mouth sweet with chloroform or sharp with A.C.E., pressured to name the child so it could at least be baptized. No.

It is fun and easy to imagine the day my great-grandmother was born, Sigga, my Sigga. Having been made two times a mother myself, it is nothing to live in the hands of it all. Nothing to feel the immense pressure of life emerging having taken over the early curiosity and then worry and excitement; the immense pressure of life emerging, stepping forward past the shock of labour, through irritation, and pain, and bargaining, and exhaustion, and abandonment—oh, God, I am the only one now. Immense pressure demands to be met with focus and determination, some conditioning toward the relentlessness to come, I think. The cleave and stretch. The no and the yes and the get out and the please and the please and the please. I'll be good. Please. And the nothing that is out of time and still, without breath. And then the release that feels like relief. Just one breath and hold it. The slick of the babe through your hands brought to the quake of your body, not yet adjusted to the idea that she is here, arrived to you. Not yet ready to release the interface of vessels and faith that were your primary service to that child, this baby.

— Oh! It's a baby. I recognize the shape of this heel. I know this baby.

Nothing to imagine in the feeling of all that. But this time, I am not to be birthing. What is it, then, to imagine into being born. Two pounds, one ounce, birthed in the middle of this prairie that draws land together in every direction.

Oh, I see. That is not difficult to imagine either. The drive and crush of it all. The forward and back of it, forward and back. The just a little more of it and again. The dark and the pressure—oh, God, I am the only one now. Blood supply interrupted. Hard going now. The whole up and dip of it. The curl and turn of it. Pressing against the threshold, some conditioning toward the relentlessness to come. Nothing to imagine at all.

In birth, life is not simply what happens next. No one's first breath happens by accident. The intention around that breath, to prise open the lungs, its lobes, lopsided though they are, to nestle the heart, opening the bronchi, the bronchioles, impossibly tiny and thinned to near invisibility with a good breath: the alveoli, where the oxygen in those millions of tiny clusters passes through the adjacent walls of minuscule air sac; and tiny capillary, where the carbon dioxide in the blood does the same. We breathe to fill the whole damn tree of it. It is easy to imagine how the force of will required to do that for the first time is immense. Oh. No. Wait.

There's something coming. It's not will.

In the body we each have a respiratory system, the whole damn tree of it. We respire. We breathe. Each of our cells does the same, each cell takes in a little oxygen, mixes it with a little food and makes ATP, this microscopic molecule we need in order to bring our muscles to bear on a situation, or to think, or take in the sense beneath our fingertips.

—Remember this.

Everyday our cells respire so much they make our entire body's weight worth of adenosine triphosphate. With it we do. We live. We become who we are. For the most part, our cells just do that work of making life's currency. They need us to collect the oxygen and release the carbon dioxide. They need us to eat and to rest. They produce when the morning is spacious and possible—hands to the hide, it is sunny today and crisp. Fresh. They produce when the moment is impossible.

—No, Leifi, it is too soon.

When we are pressed in upon. When we push back. Push.

The cells do.

We be.

The cells do, and we be, free to make our mark upon the world. But, first, we must breathe.

Respire.

The whole damn tree of it.

We must open ourselves.

We must release.

We must open again.

The whole damn tree of it.

That very first breath is the first time we surrender to the world we've been born to. The fluid we know is removed through blood and lymph, sacs kept from sticking shut by surfactant, a system of airways so elegant and intricate, so efficient a use of space that were we to flay our adult lungs open completely, we would find ourselves sliding on a surface as large as a tennis court.

In utero, fetuses develop a bypass mechanism along with the heart. Because oxygenation happens at the placenta, and because oxygen comes no other way, in utero the heart has no need of the lungs. The blood goes from pulmonary artery to descending aorta. But, once a babe is born, placenta no longer, the heart must change course. A newborn's first breath signals the heart to close its direct line between go and go again, and with that, two are made of one.

—Breathe. You must remember to breathe.

—I remember. But I can't. I can't breathe.

I had terrible asthma growing up. I remember my aunties, my father's sisters, making several teas, some more effective than others. I remember a phys-ed teacher once showing me to lift my arms above my head and breathe out. It's almost impossible to take a breath in, she told me, but there is always a little air you can push out. Make some space. When I have need, I breathe out in just that way, to this day. Make space for the salbutamol. Make space for the mometasone furoate. Make space for vapours of cardamom. Make space. Make space. Make space.

—Remember this.

Respire is a verb that traces its line back through the Old French *respirer* in the twelfth century, to the Latin *respirare* from re- "again" + *spirare* "to breathe" which, in turn, is cousin to spirit, spiritus—the breath of God. Or, stripped of its deific overtones, spiritus is life itself. We are merely the vessels that hold and bring animation to it. That first breath has nothing to do with will. Breathe in. Open (the whole damn tree of it) to life. That moment we declare ourselves present is an act of inspiration. Our very first one. So vital and then so easily forgotten.

Inhale. Exhale. Inhale. Exhale. Around sixteen times in a minute, 23,000 per day.

Some 672,000,000 in a nice long lifetime.

Oma Sigga took her very first breath in unlikely circumstances.

I am told Sigga, my Sigga, had a difficult life.

I am told she worked as hard as she could. I am told she was wonderful. A miracle. I am told something broke in her. I am told my Sigga had a long fight with an unkind mind—me too, me too.

I know we have no say in how we come about the scents and flavours of our selves. The taste of home steeped into our cells by all that is carried and passed hand-to-hand all along the ladder of how we came to be. I don't know what made my mother or father, my aunties, or my Oma Sigga. And, truth-be-told, I can only imagine and speculate on what they've made of me.

There's cardamom in the cookies.

There's cardamom in the tea.

There is cardamom in the meat.

This is the cardamom. Me.

I wonder if my Sigga imagined the many ways she might have applied her hand in bringing about her expiration. That final breath, slipping out between the folds. Was she lonely, I wonder. Would it hurt? Could it have gone some other way? Probably not. I wonder. Would she have used pills? Would she have jumped? A gun? No. Nothing that noisy. Head in the oven.

I can imagine that, too.

I have to.

Remember this.

Me too. Me too.

I'm remembering now a story about cancer and just called my mom to double-check. It was that. Though my Sigga died of bowel cancer, what persists is some strong story that she would have gone much sooner if she could have. My mother has clear memories of her Oma, my Sigga, making convincing statements of her imminent death. Not only from a part of her that may have wished for death to come, but, in my mom's telling, from a part, a fearful part, that saw death clear on the horizon— me too, me too. I wonder if that remained true throughout the length of her life. I wonder what tipped her off. Maybe the dense fog lifted at times, even after it socked her in.

I can imagine that, too.

I have to. I am too much in the inheritance of my family lines, too much in danger of replicating them, too much a mother not to.

The story of it all, the whole damn tree of it, needs to be burned, as far as I am concerned. Being in a body. Life that gives. Life that takes away. Life that gives again. All maternity is trial by fire. It is dressed up in its pinks and blues and soft edges and billowing curtains. It is made firm, a pillar to what we can spend on it, with little true sense of what it might cost. And, even in hindsight, trying as hard as we can to deny it, there is something, even just a little something about life that can only be received, that can be met at the door, greeted or repelled. But there is a threshold and something will cross, someone will carry through, something will live or die. Someone. Some air-breathing being, some three cells in a cave. We may have some say in setting the sequence, we may even stack the odds, but some measure of consequence meets us. There. At the door. Open or closed. Lights on. Lights off. Polite knock or battering ram. We meet. We are met. We meet again. In moments so fast we can barely keep from storying over, around, and through them. Moments so fast, we don't even know they have happened. Salts and metals so incendiary we are unlikely to catch glimpse of the flame, to know blue from purple from green from white. But we have a good sense of the before and a good sense of the after, and the mind needs no imagination to connect any dots it rests upon.

In this way, death begets life. The tender inheritance of each new generation.

For all her courage and strength, the whole tall tree of her in full leaf, Sigga, my Sigga, could not bear the heavy wet weight of so many snap autumnal snows. All her possible births.

All her possible deaths. It serves me to imagine them, too.

Remember this.

The breath.

Contributors

Colleen Abel is a disabled writer living in the Midwest. Her work has appeared in venues such as *Lit Hub, Cincinnati Review, The Southern Review, Colorado Review, Pleiades,* and elsewhere. Her first poetry collection, *Remake,* won the 2015 Editors Prize from Unicorn Press. She has two chapbooks, *Housewifery* and *Deviants,* a hybrid work that won Sundress Publications' 2016 Chapbook Prize. She has been awarded fellowships from University of Wisconsin-Madison's Institute for Creative Writing and the Tulsa Artist Fellowship. She is an assistant professor of English at Eastern Illinois University and the editor of *Bluestem Magazine.*

Sarah Allen is a poet and author of books for young readers. Her first book, *What Stars Are Made Of,* was an ALA Notable Book of 2020 and her second, *Breathing Underwater,* is a Junior Library Guild Selection for 2021. She received her MFA from Brigham Young University and has had poetry published in *The Evansville Review, Quarter After Eight, Tipton Poetry Journal,* and more. She spends her non-writing time watching David Attenborough documentaries and singing show-tunes too loudly. Find her online @sarahallenbooks.

Latif Askia Ba is a poet with choreic cerebral palsy from Brooklyn & Staten Island, New York. He's currently living on the Upper West Side, working on an MFA in creative writing at Columbia University. The bulk of his work explores the culture, language, and philosophy of disability.

Zan Bockes is a direct descendent of Bacchus, the Roman god of wine and revelry. She earned an MFA in creative writing from the University of Montana. Her fiction, nonfiction, and poetry have appeared in many magazines and anthologies, including *Writers and Their Notebooks*, *The Pedestal Magazine*, *Out of Our*, *Cutbank*, and *Phantasmagoria*, and she has had four nominations for the Pushcart Prize. Her first collection of poetry, *Caught in Passing*, came out in 2013, and another collection, *Alibi for Stolen Light*, was published in 2018.

Rebecca Burke (*Editor*) is a graduate of George Mason University's MFA program in creative writing. As a graduate student, she served as the submissions and acquisitions manager at Stillhouse Press and as the fiction editor at *So to Speak Journal*. She is currently working on her first book, a novel about PTSD, queerness, and navigating childhood trauma. You can find her on Twitter @BeccaBurke95 and learn more about all the projects she's involved with at rrburkewrites.com.

Becca Carson is a queer poet, artist, and high school creative writing teacher and staff adviser of the Aerie Literary Magazine Program. She lives in Missoula, Montana with her wife and kids. When she isn't writing or creating things she likes to read, travel, and explore outdoors. She is the author of *Flight Path*, her first book of poems.

Rob Colgate is a Filipino-American poet from Evanston, Illinois. He holds a degree in psychology from Yale University and an MFA in poetry from the New Writers Project at The University of Texas at Austin. A Pushcart nominee, his work appears or is forthcoming in *Best New Poets*, *Prairie Schooner*, *Washington Square Review*, *Muzzle*, and *Adroit*, among others. He is the winner of the 2022 Andrew Julius Gutow Poetry Prize and serves as assistant poetry editor at *Foglifter Journal*. Currently, he is a Fulbright scholar conducting research and writing poetry at Toronto Metropolitan University's School of Disability Studies.

Willy Conley, born profoundly deaf, is an award-winning writer and photographer. His work has been produced internationally and published widely in anthologies and periodicals. He is a recipient of a PEW/National Theatre Artist Residency grant and the 2007-2008 Schaefer Professorship. Conley is a graduate of the Rochester Institute of Technology, Boston University, and Towson University. He is a retired professor and former chairperson of Theatre and Dance at Gallaudet University in Washington, DC. He is the author of *The World of White Water*, *Visual-Gestural Communication*, *Listening Through the Bone*, *The Deaf Heart*, and *Vignettes of the Deaf Character and Other Plays*.

C.M. Crockford is an autistic/ADHD writer whose work has been featured in the *Wingless Dreamer Spring Anthology*, *Vast Chasm*, and *No Cinema! Quarterly* among others. He's published two chapbooks, including *Mark The Place* with Thirty West Publishing. Crockford lives in Philadelphia with his cats but has been all over. You can find more of his poetry, essays, and stories on www.cmcrockford.com.

Alton Melvar M Dapanas *(they/them)*, a native of southern Philippines, is the author of *Towards a Theory on City Boys: Prose Poems* (UK: Newcomer Press, 2021) and *dîlî ingon nátô / not like us* (US: forthcoming). Published in Sweden, Lebanon, Germany, Taiwan, Austria, Nigeria, Japan, and the Netherlands, their latest works have appeared in *Modern Poetry in Translation* (UK), *Tolka Journal* (Ireland), *New Contrast* (South Africa), *The Best Asian Poetry* (Singapore), *Mekong Review* (Australia), *Canthius Magazine* (Canada), and *Poetry Lab Shanghai* (China) where they were translated into the Chinese. They're editor-at-large at *Asymptote Journal*, assistant nonfiction editor at *Panorama: The Journal of Intelligent Travel* and *Atlas & Alice Literary Magazine*, and reader at *Creative Nonfiction* magazine. Find more at https://linktr.ee/samdapanas.

Arria Deepwater (*she/they*) identifies as chronically ill & disabled, queer, feminist, female, cis- and white-presenting and faithfully middle-aged. When she is able to write, she focuses on short stories, guided meditations, and nurturing a few story-babies into long format pieces. Her work often explores intersections between human limitation, culture, ecology, and spiritual understanding. She lives and works near Kingston, Ontario, Canada; the unceded territory of the Omàmìwininì Algonquin People. There, Arria shares a house-on-a-lake with her mother and their ridiculously adorable dog (her mother is pretty cute too). www.arriadeepwater.com

Rhea Dhanbhoora lives and writes in Upstate New York. Her work has appeared or is forthcoming in various publications including *Chronogram, Peripheries Journal, Capsule Stories, The Spill,* and *JMWW*. She's currently on the board for the literary organization, Quiet Lightning, and is working on several projects, among which is a linked collection of stories about women, based in the Parsi Zoroastrian diaspora. Her chapbook, *Sandalwood-Scented Skeletons*, is available with Finishing Line Press. Follow her work at rheadhanbhoora.com.

Kara Dorris is the author of two poetry collections: *Have Ruin, Will Travel* (2019) and *When the Body is a Guardrail* (2020) from Finishing Line Press. She has also published five chapbooks. Her poetry has appeared in *Prairie Schooner, DIAGRAM, Hayden's Ferry Review, Tinderbox, Puerto del Sol,* and *Crazyhorse*, among others literary journals, as well as the anthology *Beauty is a Verb* (2011). Her prose has appeared in *Waxwing* and the anthology *The Right Way to be Crippled and Naked* (2016). For more information, please visit karadorris.com.

Anesce Dremen is a US travel writer. A first-generation college student and domestic violence survivor, she studied in four cities in China with the support of the Critical Language Scholarship and the Benjamin A. Gilman Scholarship. Her work has been published in *Persephone's Daughters, Tiny Spoon, Tea Journey, The Bombay Literary Magazine, Shanghai Poetry Lab, T Ching*, and *The Isolation Journals*, among others. She is a 2022 Fulbright-Nehru ETA in Kolkata, India. Anesce is often found with a tea cup in hand, traveling between the US, China, and India. She is the international coordinator of The Quarantine Train. You can find her on social media @WritersDremen.

Nathan Viktor Fawaz is a writer, artist, and parent specializing in speculative nonfiction and automythography. The themes that saturate their work and life include: memory, trauma, embodimindment, lineage, mythology, and liberation. They hold an MFA in creative writing from the University of British Columbia and are currently pursuing a PhD at the University of Alberta.

Vanessa Garza is a survivor of a rare neurovascular malformation (AVM) which led to multiple brain surgeries and epilepsy. She holds a degree in finance and government from the University of Notre Dame and worked in the corporate arena for nearly fifteen years, up to her diagnosis. To find peace in her health trauma, she transitioned from consultant to essayist, finally pursuing a long-lived passion for writing. A South Texas native, Vanessa currently lives in Boston with her husband and two children, and she recently graduated from GrubStreet's Intensive Essay Incubator Program.

Cristina Hartmann is a Brazilian-American writer living in Pittsburgh. Born profoundly deaf and becoming DeafBlind later in life, her stories explore identity and relationships through disability and immigrant experiences. Her work has appeared or is forthcoming in *McSweeney's, The MacGuffin, descant, Kaleidoscope*, and other publications. She enjoys scarves, cheap port, and first-person narratives.

Duane L. Herrmann, father, grandfather, internationally published, award-winning poet and historian, has had work translated into several languages, in print and online. He has a sci-fi novel, *Escape from Earth*, seven collections of poetry, and more chapbooks. His poetry has received the Robert Hayden Poetry Fellowship, inclusion in *American Poets of the 1990s*, Map of Kansas Literature (website), Kansas Poets Trail, and others. His history, *By Thy Strengthening Grace*, received the Ferguson Kansas History Book Award. These accomplishments defy his traumatic childhood embellished by dyslexia, ADHD, and, now, PTSD. He spends his time on the prairie with trees in the breeze and writes—and loves the light of the moon!

Natalie E. Illum is a poet, disability activist and singer living in Washington, DC. She is the recipient of four Poetry Fellowship Grants from the DC Arts Commission and a former Jenny McKean Moore Fellow. She was a founding board member of mothertongue, an LGBTQA open mic that lasted fifteen years. She competed on the National Poetry Slam circuit and was the 2013 Beltway Grand Slam Champion. Her work has appeared in various publications, and on NPR's *Snap Judgement*. Natalie has an MFA in creative writing from American University and was a Teaching Artist for Poetry Out Loud. You can find her on Instagram and Twitter as @poetryrox, and as one half of the band All Her Muses.

Jill Rachel Jacobs' commentaries, features, and essays have been published in *The Washington Post*, *The New York Times*, *Reuters*, *The Boston Globe*, *The San Francisco Chronicle*, *The NY Post*, *The Huffington Post*, *The Philadelphia Inquirer*, *Newsday*, and *The Independent*. Ms. Jacobs has interviewed noted actors, musicians, and humanitarians including Glenn Close, Jessica Lange, Bette Midler, Dick Van Dyke, Tom Selleck, Ted Danson, Mary Tyler Moore, Jane Goodall, Gabriel Bryne, Carrie

Fisher, and Herbie Hancock. Ms. Jacobs is a Pushcart nominated poet whose poetry has been featured in *Lost Coast Review*, *The Tower Journal*, *Muddy River Poetry Review*, *Varnish Journal*, *The Pomona Review*, and *Ygdrasil: A Journal of The Poetic Arts*.

Kimberly Jae is an award-winning slam poet ranking in the top 30 slam poets in the world by PSI in 2018. In 2019, she survived a stroke leading to physical disability and aphasia, a language-based disability affecting her ability to read, write, and speak. Undaunted, she has since won fellowships, competitions (making it to Nationals in multiple countries), and has been published including in *Alt Minds Literary Magazine* (Canada), *Hawai'i Review* (US), and anthologies, including *In the Shadow of the Mic: Three Decades of Slam Poetry in Pittsburgh*.

Zoë Luh (*she/they*) is a poet and artist. She studied comparative American studies at Oberlin College, where she was also part of Oberlin's slam poetry team, OSLAM, for three years. Zoë published her first book of poetry, *[and time erodes like thunder]*, with Assure Press in the spring of 2020, and has published several opinions articles with the *Oberlin Review*. In her free time, she loves to read, paint, and cook with friends. Zoë is a Gemini sun and moon, and a Scorpio rising.

Elizabeth Meade is a poet with cerebral palsy who lives in Asheville, North Carolina. Born against the odds of survival at 23.5 weeks, she weighed just 1.1 pounds. This miracle inspires her enthusiastic exploration of life, immense gratitude, and compassionate heart. She began writing poetry when she was fourteen, shortly after she inexplicably lost her ability to walk. She enjoys reciting her poetry, traveling, connecting with people, animals, and nature, as well as writing the occasional song. Her poems have appeared in the magazines *Kaleidoscope* and *The Laurel of Asheville*. She is currently working on her first book of poems.

Zackary Medlin *(he/him)* grew up in South Carolina, ran away to Alaska, tried his luck in Utah, and now lives in Colorado, where he teaches at Fort Lewis College. He is the winner of the Nancy D. Hargrove Editor's Choice Prize, the Patricia Goedicke Prize in Poetry, and a recipient of an AWP Intro Journals Award. He holds an MFA from the University of Alaska Fairbanks and a PhD from the University of Utah, where he was awarded a Clarence Snow Fellowship. His poetry has appeared in journals such as *Colorado Review*, *The Cincinnati Review*, *Grist*, and more.

Teresa Milbrodt is the author of three short story collections: *Instances of Head-Switching*, *Bearded Women: Stories*, and *Work Opportunities*. She has also published a novel, *The Patron Saint of Unattractive People*, and a flash fiction collection, *Larissa Takes Flight: Stories*. Her fiction, creative nonfiction, and poetry have appeared in numerous literary magazines, and her work has been nominated for a Pushcart Prize and Best of the Net award. Milbrodt lives in Salem, Virginia, where she is an Assistant Professor of Creative Writing at Roanoke College. She believes in coffee, long walks with her MP3 player, and writing the occasional haiku. Read more of her work at: http://teresamilbrodt.com/homepage/.

Laura Mulqueen was born in Huntsville, Alabama and received her MA from Auburn University in 2020. She currently works as a technical writer and has taught English, composition, and yoga, along with serving as an editor for *Southern Humanities Review*. Her work has appeared in *Wilderness House Literature Review* and she has had poetry recognized by the Academy of American Poets' Robert Hughes Mount Jr. Prize. She lives in Birmingham, Alabama with her son.

Chisom Okafor is a Nigerian poet and clinical nutritionist. His debut full-length poetry manuscript, *Birthing*, was a finalist for the Sillerman First Book Prize for African Poets.

Kaleigh O'Keefe (*they/them*) is a gender outlaw and proud union member living in Dorchester, Massachusetts. Their poetry has appeared in *Breaking the Chains: a Socialist Perspective on Women's Liberation*, Kissing *Dynamite, Button Poetry*, won the PRIDE Poetry Prize in *Passengers Journal*, and is featured on indie music legend Ceschi's album *Sans Soleil*. Kaleigh is a contributor and editor for *Liberation News*, co-founder of Game Over Books, and host of the First Fridays Youth Open Mic in Jamaica Plain. You can find them at www.kaleighokeefe.com and @KaleighOKeefeOK.

Cynthia Romanowski is a disabled interdisciplinary artist (writing, drawing, and performance prose). Her fiction explores the lived experience of trauma and mental illness. Her short stories, articles, and essays have appeared in *Coast Magazine, The Weekly Rumpus, The Nervous Breakdown, Angels Flight Literary West, Writers Resist*, and on the podcast *No Extra Words*. She holds an MFA in fiction from University of California, Riverside's low-res program in Palm Desert and is a former editor of *The Coachella Review*. She lives in her hometown of Huntington Beach and is currently working on a coming-of-age memoir about spirituality and mental illness.

Lili Sarayrah is a Jordanian-American violinist and storyteller who performs all over the world. She began writing to manage her chronic pain and loves reading, traveling, and bargaining. lilisarayrah.com.

Jess Skyleson is an autistic cancer survivor and a former aerospace engineer who began composing poetry after being diagnosed with stage IV cancer at age thirty-nine. Currently in remission, they are now exploring new potential paths in creative writing. They were awarded the 2022 Hippocrates Poetry and Medicine Prize, received an Honorable Mention in the Tor House Poetry Prize, and were a finalist for the *Yemassee* Poetry Prize. Their work has appeared in *Oberon Poetry Magazine*, *Nixes Mate Review*, and *Ponder Review*, among others, and will be included in upcoming anthologies from Stone Poetry Quarterly and Fly on the Wall Press.

Wendy Elizabeth Wallace (*she/her*) is a queer writer with vision loss. She grew up in Buffalo, New York, and has now landed in Connecticut by way of Pennsylvania, Berlin, Heidelberg, and Indiana. She is the co-founding editor of *Peatsmoke: A Literary Journal* and met the kind people who suffer through her rough drafts at the Purdue University MFA. Her work has appeared in *The Rumpus*, *Willow Springs*, *Hobart Pulp*, *Pithead Chapel*, *The Los Angeles Review*, and elsewhere. Find her on Twitter @WendyEWallace1 or at www.wendywallacewriter.com.

Tessa Weber loves all things literary and dogs. She is originally from a suburb of Minneapolis, Minnesota and currently lives in the Boston, Massachusetts area. She is pursuing her Master of Arts in English at the University of Massachusetts, Boston. She works taking care of patients during the day, and weaves in writing and creative arts during the rest. She can be seen on her blog cfgivesmecrazyhair.com and soon to be published in "Write on the DOT," a Dorchester and UMass Boston MFA affiliated writing series. She is currently working on a young adult prose piece, a memoir, and collaborative nonfiction book.

Ann Zuccardy is a thirty-year paid writing veteran, two-time TEDx speaker, adjunct professor, keynote speaker, traumatic brain injury survivor, life coach, and advocate. She loves neuroplasticity and cupcakes.

Acknowledgments

We thank the following publishers for providing homes to these previously published pieces included within this anthology:

Adelaide Literary Magazine, issue 28, September 2019: "My Father's Feet" by Ann Zuccardy

Breakwater Review, issue 26: "My Mania as an Alaskan Summer" by Zackary Medlin

Growing Up Girl: An Anthology of Voices from Marginalized Spaces edited by Michelle Sewell (GirlChild Press, 2006): "My Mother's Prayer" by Natalie E. Illum

Nevertheless Away, blog: portions of "Hairline Movement" by Anesce Dremen

Peatsmoke Journal, Spring 2021 issue: "Carnaval, Upstate" by Cristina Hartmann

Pembroke Magazine, No. 51: "You May Mistake This for A Love Story" by Teresa Milbrodt

Punk Noir Magazine, May 2021: "j.r. borja bridge, 2019" by Alton Melvar M. Dapanas

Sexy Like Us: Disability, Humor, and Sexuality by Teresa Milbrodt (University Press of Mississippi, 2022): sections of "Cyclops Notes"

The New Orleans Review, issue 46: "Your Very Own Low-Vision Dating Adventure" by Wendy Elizabeth Wallace, under the title "Choose Your Own Low-Vision Dating Adventure"

Notre Dame Magazine, Spring 2022: "When My Broken Brain Misfires" by Vanessa R. Garza

The Machine Code of a Bleeding Moon by Latif Askia Ba (Stillhouse Press, 2022): "On Gospel (a meander)," "Houses," "Bájalo," and "The Dentist's Caliphate"

The Santa Fe Writers Project Quarterly, issue 29, 2022: "Diagnoses and Misdiagnoses (alphabetical, incomplete)" and "Diagnostic Laparoscopy" by Kaleigh O'Keefe

The Weekly Rumpus, 2014: "Live Action Regret" by Cynthia Romanowski

The Whistling Fire, 2013: "Wrestle Mania" by Cynthia Romanowski

The World of White Water by Willy Conley (Kelsay Books, 2021): "The Galvanic Skin Response Test"

This book would not have been possible
without the hard work of our staff.

We would like to acknowledge:

Amanda Ganus	Assistant Editor/Nonfiction Editor
Natalie Plahuta	Nonfiction Editor
Lisa DesRochers-Short	Poetry Editor
Lee Tury	Poetry Editor
Bareerah Y. Ghani	Fiction Editor
Emilie Knudsen	Fiction Editor
Hannah Dobrick	Fiction Editor
Brittney Burdick	Fiction Editor
Scott Berg	Stillhouse Press Publisher
Linda Hall	Operations Manager
Alex Horn	Director of Media & Marketing
Virginia Eggerton	Jacket Designer
Reina Hudspeth	Cover Artist

Readers

Abigail Casas	Mary Winsor
Casper Brooks	Sarah Gheyas
Ethan Reynolds	Shannon Richardson
Julia Swistara	Tanika Thomas
Kate Steagall	

STILL
HOUSE
PRESS

CPSIA information can be obtained
at www.ICGtesting.com
Printed in the USA
LVHW082350020723
751382LV00002BA/175